ONIONS AND GARLIC

Edible

Series Editor: Andrew F. Smith

EDIBLE is a revolutionary series of books dedicated to food and drink that explores the rich history of cuisine. Each book reveals the global history and culture of one type of food or beverage.

Already published

Onions and Garlic

A Global History

Martha Jay

REAKTION BOOKS

Published by Reaktion Books Ltd
Unit 32, Waterside
44–48 Wharf Road
London N1 7UX, UK
www.reaktionbooks.co.uk

First published 2016

Copyright © Martha Jay 2016

All rights reserved
No part of this publication may be reproduced, stored in a retrieval
system, or transmitted, in any form or by any means, electronic,
mechanical, photocopying, recording or otherwise, without the prior
permission of the publishers

Printed and bound in China by 1010 Printing International Ltd

A catalogue record for this book is available from the British Library

ISBN 978 1 78023 587 5

Contents

Introduction

> When the Devil's left foot touched soil outside the Garden of
> Eden, garlic sprang up, and his right gave rise to onions.
> Islamic proverb

From the silky slipperiness of a chopped onion in a soup to
the perfume of garlic in a tomato sauce, onions and garlic
seem to be an integral part of cooking. They're the vegetables
I reach for the most often; hardly a day goes by that I do not
chop an onion to throw into a soup or sauce, or crush some
garlic to add to pasta or a dish of stir-fried vegetables. Yet they
are rarely the stars of the show. Although they have a fair claim
to be the most eaten foodstuff in the world – according to the
UN, 175 countries around the world produce an onion crop, far
more than grow wheat – countless recipe books warn against
letting the natural pungency of onions or garlic overwhelm
the other ingredients of a dish for fear of giving diners the
dreaded onion breath.

But the story of the humble onion, ever present but
unsung, goes far beyond food. As I delved further into onion
lore, I discovered that its history also includes folklore, science
and art. Why do onions make us cry, and can we do anything
about it? Why do they say that garlic will protect us from
vampires? How do you use onions to predict the weather?

Does taking garlic pills mean that we'll avoid heart disease? And who brought the leek to Wales? They've entered the lexicons of many languages, too; from the English 'know your onions' to the French *s'occuper ses oignons*, meaning to look after one's own onions; in other words, to mind one's own business. A forgetful person in Portugal is a *cabeça d'alho xoxo*, or head of rotten garlic; in China, 'chicken feathers and garlic skin' is a phrase used to describe things that are worthless, since they are the inedible bits left over from preparing a meal; and in Japan, 'a duck that comes bearing green onions' is a phrase used to describe something that's proved unexpectedly useful or fortunate.

Garlic, leeks, chives, onions, spring onions (scallions) and shallots all taste slightly different, but they are all members of the same family – the allium family – which has been a friend to mankind since the earliest times. In their almost infinite variety, they have spread across the world, adding sweetness

Onion market in Khartoum, Sudan, 1936.

Office of War Information poster, UK, 1941–5.

and pungency to dishes ranging from French onion soup to hamburgers to Korean pickled garlic.

The onion is one of the oldest domesticated vegetables in existence. Humans were probably eating onions even before they ate grain: wild allium varieties have been foraged since ancient times. As humans began to eschew the nomadic life and become settlers, we started to practise agriculture by selecting edible plants from the wild and transferring them to plots in order to cultivate and harvest them. Traces of alliums have been found in the remains of Bronze Age settlements, though it's not clear whether these were domesticated types. Early farmers selected the plants that formed the largest, quickest-growing bulbs, and as these plants fertilized one another in their plots, plants more and more like our modern onion, with its large, sweet bulb, were developed. In this way, in Central Asia, the domesticated onion, which we now know by the Latin binomial *Allium cepa*, was born – and it soon began to spread. At first it was brought to the Middle East by traders, and from there it made its way across the world.

There are between 500 and 650 varieties of allium world-wide, including ornamental varieties. Of these, there are seven major species of edible allium crop, the most common of which in the West is probably *A. cepa* (*cepa* is Latin for onion, and from it are derived the Spanish *cebolla* and the Polish *cibula*, among others). This is the large-bulbed kind of allium, the kind we would familiarly call 'onion' rather than garlic or leek and from which many varieties, including shallots, derive. These are hugely varied in size and shape; the bulbs can be as tiny as a couple of millimetres across. The world's largest recorded onion was grown by one Peter Glazebrook of Newark, Nottinghamshire, in 2012; it weighed a huge 18 lb 1 oz (8.19 kg), smashing his previous world record by 2 oz (56 g). He stated proudly: 'It would certainly do for a lot of hotdogs.'[1]

The formation of the onion's bulb happens when the plant is exposed to an adequate number of hours of sunlight at a certain temperature. Carbohydrate is produced by the onion's leaves through photosynthesis and stored in the base; essentially, onion bulbs are just tightly packed leaf bases, a fact that accounts for their many layers. *A. cepa* varieties can be divided into long-day and short-day onions. Long-day onions must be exposed to fourteen hours of sunlight a day to grow, and are often grown in the northern hemisphere. They grow over the summer and are harvested in the autumn. Short-day onions, which need between twelve and fourteen hours of light a day in order to form bulbs, are grown in warmer places, such as equatorial regions, where they can be planted in the autumn and overwintered to be harvested in the spring.

But not all allium varieties form bulbs. The second main variety of edible allium crop, chives (*A. schoenoprasum*), grows rather differently, as bunches of furled leaves that look rather like hollow stems, usually with purple or white flowers. Chives are the most widespread group of allium plants around the world, and can even be found in Antarctica and in arctic regions as high as 70°N.[2] In more temperate climates, they grow in moist soil and on mountainsides.

The third kind, Chinese chives (*A. tuberosum*), which look much like chives since they also grow as bunches of leaves, grow wild all over East Asia from Mongolia to the Philippines.[3]

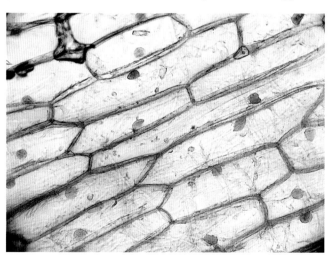

Onion cells stained with methylene blue so that the nuclei are visible. Each layer of an onion, a leaf base storing carbohydrate, is just one cell thick.

They are also known as 'garlic chives' and have a more pungent, garlicky taste. Their flowers can be eaten too.

The fourth category of allium plants is garlic (*A. sativum*), which grows in heads made up of a number of segments called cloves. Recent research suggests that garlic comes from further east than *A. cepa*, in Central Asia on the northwestern side of the Tian Shan Mountains, near Kyrgyzstan. It was introduced into China from Central Asia and into Japan from Korea, where it has a long history stretching back to at least 400 BCE. It reproduces asexually rather than from seed; if you plant one of the cloves, it will grow into a garlic plant. The fermented black garlic used in Asian cuisine is not a different species, but is black as a result of the process of fermentation (although, confusingly, there is another plant called 'black garlic', which is indeed a different species, as well as *A. nigrum*, an ornamental variety.)

Members of the *A. ampeloprasum* group of species – which includes the leek, the national symbol of Wales – don't generally bulb. Instead, they have a stem-like formation of

Chive (*Allium schoenoprasum*) flowers.

W. G. Smith, Del. e Lith

Flowerheads of a leek (*Allium ampeloprasum*) and sandleek (*A. scorodoprasum*).
Coloured lithograph by W. G. Smith, *c.* 1863, after himself.

Liliaceae.

121. A. *Allium ursinum L.* Bären-Lauch.

B. *Allium nigrum L.* Schwarzer Lauch.

Allium ursinum and *A. nigrum*, from a German horticultural book of 1903.

tightly wrapped leaves. Elephant garlic, despite its appearance, is also a member of this group, as is the pearl onion.

The bunching onion, *A. fistulosum*, is the most popular vegetable of Japan and looks rather like the missing link between the leek and the spring onion. The name of the species means 'tubular', and when you cut into the green part at the top it is hollow inside. Historically it is the main allium vegetable of China (where it is known as *cong* – what Westerners call 'onions', the Chinese call *yang cong*, or 'foreign onions') and Japan (*negi*), and is thought to have been cultivated there for more than 2,000 years.[4] *A. fistulosum* is also known as the Welsh onion, but not because it comes from Wales: the name comes from the Anglo-Saxon word *welise*, meaning 'foreign'.[5] It found its way to Europe during the Middle Ages, but has never toppled the traditional European favourites of onion and garlic.

A. oschaninii is the French grey shallot or griselle, which is sometimes known as the 'true shallot' to distinguish it from what we familiarly call a shallot, which is actually a kind of *A. cepa*. It grows mainly in Central Asia. And the last of the major groups of edible alliums is *A. chinense*, also known as *rakkyo*, a popular East Asian bunching type of onion with clusters of very small bulbs that are often eaten pickled.

Of course, there are also hundreds of other varieties – meadow leeks, ramps, wild garlic – and probably some that haven't yet been discovered. This is the story of one of the world's favourite vegetable families, a story of fine cuisine and art, peasants and kings, conquest and colonization, vampires and mummies, magic and medicine. But most of all, it's the story of an ordinary vegetable.

I

The Ancient Allium

I cannot imagine a civilization without onions.
Julia Child

From their beginning in the mountains of Central Asia, onions
and other alliums spread quickly across the ancient world.
Easy to grow and to store, they found their place as a staple
of many civilizations.

The story of alliums and civilization starts in ancient
Mesopotamia, that area between the Tigris and the Euphra-
tes that is considered the cradle of civilization and was the
home of the Akkadian, Babylonian and Assyrian empires.
Though the summers in this part of the world are hot and
rainfall during much of the year is rare, the ground is very
fertile because of the layers of sediment deposited by the two
rivers. Once irrigation was developed, this so-called Fertile
Crescent became a cornucopia of grain, livestock, date palms,
fruits and vegetables.

Much of the information we have about food culture
in ancient Mesopotamia relates to food as a commodity,
recording what was bought and sold. Cuneiform tablets provide information about produce such as grain, which could
be traded, moved and stored. Fresh vegetables leave fewer

traces, because they are often grown for use in the home rather than being traded, and therefore do not always appear in receipt books or household accounts. We do however have an invaluable record of some ancient recipes. Three cuneiform tablets known as the Yale Babylonian Tablets, which date from around 1600 BCE, list around forty recipes from ancient Mesopotamia. Onions, leeks and garlic all feature heavily in these recipes, as do the more mysterious *samidu*, *suhutinnu* and *andahsu*. Though we don't know exactly what these were, it's likely that they were also members of the allium family. The historian Jean Bottéro notes:

> It would seem that those old gourmets had discovered affinities, a complementarity of taste, among these plants, which are, moreover, usually mentioned in couples (garlic and leek, notably), so they used them most often together, like our 'fines herbes' . . . There is no compelling evidence of a belief in a 'supernatural,' or 'magical,' or religious effect in the use of these or other ingredients: it was mainly, no doubt exclusively, a matter of taste.[1]

The first tablet contains 25 recipes for broths, 21 meat-based and four vegetable-based, all of which contain some sort of allium. In most of them leeks and garlic are minced and used to flavour a sort of stock in which meat or vegetables are then cooked, just as we might start a casserole today by softening chopped onion and garlic before adding meat and stock. One example is for a broth in the 'Assyrian style':

> Meat is used. Prepare water; add fat . . ., garlic, and *zurumu* with . . . blood(?), and (mashed) leek and garlic. It is ready to serve.[2]

This late Babylonian tablet is a list of plants that can be found in the garden of a former Babylonian king, Marduk-apla-iddina II (r. 721–710 and 703–701 BCE). The first three items listed in cuneiform script in the left-hand column are garlic, onions and leeks.

The ancient Egyptians, too, ate onions: the Roman historian Herodotus reported in the fifth century BCE that the poorer people of Egypt would have bread, raw onions and beer for their midday meal, and on the wall of the Aten Temple in Karnak a workman is pictured eating that very lunch (with the addition of cucumbers). Herodotus also mentions in his *History* that on the Pyramid of Cheops, also known as the Great Pyramid of Giza, was an inscription detailing how much had been spent on radishes, onions and leeks for the workmen as it was being built in about 2550 BCE: 1,600 talents of silver. An Egyptian talent was about 27 kg (60 lb), so this is a whopping 43,200 kg of silver, which today would set you back around $21 million. The word for 'leek' in Egyptian was also the word for all vegetables, which goes to show how ubiquitous this green vegetable must have been. The historian Joan P. Alcock mentions that onions are compared in Egyptian texts to 'sound white teeth', so they were presumably a small, white variety rather than the apple-sized globes we are used to today.[3]

Onions had other meanings in Egypt, too: since the Egyptians saw the universe as being made up of concentric circles of heaven, hell and earth, the onion, with its many layers of rings, was thought to symbolize it. The onion was dedicated to the goddess Isis, patroness of nature, because it was also thought to resemble the phases of the moon when it was cut into. The Roman historian Pliny the Elder reported in his *Natural History* that garlic and onions were used by

Models of items that the rich departed of ancient Egypt would need in the afterlife – such as this clay model of a head of garlic – were interred with them in their tombs.

Egyptians rather like the orbs of kings; supposedly, an onion was held in the right hand while taking an oath of high office. No Egyptian report on this custom has been found, so it seems likely that Pliny was merely repeating hearsay aimed at ridiculing foreigners. Onions have, however, been found in tombs and in the wrappings of mummies, often placed in the armpits or groin. This may be because they were believed to have antibacterial properties, or were intended to mask unpleasant smells. Priests were forbidden to eat them.[4]

The Book of Numbers, which appears in both the Bible and the Hebrew Torah, tells how the Israelites left Egypt under Moses to find the Promised Land. While on their way they bemoan 'the fish we ate in Egypt at no cost – also the cucumbers, melons, leeks, onions and garlic' – all tasty, fresh items that could not be found in the desert, or grown by a people on the move.

Greece and Rome

The Greeks and Romans were both very fond of onions and garlic. In his *Natural History*, Pliny describes the varieties available to the Greeks:

> The Greeks have many varieties of the onion: the Sardian onion, the Samothracian, the Alsidenian, the setanian, the schistan, and the Ascalonian [shallot], so called from Ascalon, a city of Judaea. They have, all of them, a pungent smell, which draws tears from the eyes, those of Cyprus more particularly, and those of Cnidos the least of all.

He also explains that round onions are more flavourful than white ones.

The great poet Homer tells in the *Iliad* how Hecamede, the captive daughter of Arsinoos, served a potion of Pramnian wine to King Nestor with a meal: 'She first drew before the twain a table, fair, with feet of cyanus, and well-polished, and set thereon a basket of bronze, and therewith an onion, a relish for their drink, and pale honey, and ground meal of sacred barley.' Onions were often eaten with drinks, rather as we might eat olives, but they might also serve the purpose of pepping someone up before a fight. Both practices are mentioned by Socrates in around 360 BCE, around 400 years after the *Iliad*, in Xenophon's *Symposium*, albeit jokily:

> 'Gentlemen,' said Charmides, 'Niceratus is intent on going home smelling of onions to make his wife believe that no one would even have conceived the thought of kissing him.'
>
> 'Undoubtedly,' said Socrates. 'But we run the risk of getting a different sort of reputation . . . For though the onion seems to be in the truest sense a relish, since it adds to our enjoyment not only of food, but also of drink, yet if we eat it not only with our dinner but after it as well, take care that some one does not say of us that on our visit to Callias we were merely indulging our appetites.'
>
> 'Heaven forbid, Socrates!' was the reply. 'I grant that when a man is setting out for battle, it is well for him to nibble an onion, just as some people give their game-cocks a feed of garlic before pitting them together in the ring; as for us, however, our plans perhaps look more to getting a kiss from some one than to fighting.'

Athletes in the Olympic Games ate garlic, and were rubbed down with it, before competing.

Socrates' terrifying and austere republic, as outlined by Plato, allows its inhabitants the staple foods of corn, barley and wheat. In this dialogue Socrates is depicted as considerably less of a joker, but although he is extremely sniffy about such luxuries as sofas, cakes and perfume, and believes such entertainments as singing and poetry to be positively corrupting, the people's diet is not restricted to staples alone: 'of course they will have a relish – salt, and olives, and cheese, and onions.' Onions in ancient Greece were clearly considered tasty, but hardly decadent, and were available to everyone. They were turned to more poetic uses by Homer in the *Odyssey*, written at the end of the eighth century BCE: the hero Odysseus' tunic is described as 'all shining as is the sheen upon the skin of a dried onion, so soft it was'.

Garlic may have bordered on the magical, too. In the tenth book of the *Odyssey*, the gods' messenger, Hermes, gives a herb 'grown from the blood of the Gigante killed in the isle

Corinthian terracotta figure of a mule carrying a pestle and mortar containing cheese and a bunch of garlic, *c.* 360 BCE.

Mary Delany, *Allium moly*, 1779. Delany identifies this flower as *moly*, the magical herb that helped Odysseus in Homer's epic poem.

of Circe' to Odysseus to protect him from the magic of the goddess Circe, who has bewitched his friends and turned them into pigs. This plant, named *moly*, has a flower 'white as milk'. Various candidates for *moly* have been proffered, one of which is a kind of wild garlic. The sixteenth-century English herbalist John Gerard certainly thought this was what Homer meant, identifying seven different *moly*s, and one – *Moly Homericum* – that he thought was the magical herb in question.

The Greek playwright Aristophanes often referred to garlic and onions in his comedies, usually in reference to his characters' personal hygiene. In *The Knights*, a satire of 424 BCE, a sausage-seller is encouraged to swallow a few cloves of garlic before a battle to give him 'greater mettle for the fight', just as the game-cocks were in Xenophon's *Symposium* (or, presumably, at least to put the ravening hordes off coming into close contact with him). The name we now use for the onion family, 'allium', is said to come from the Greek αλεω, 'to avoid', because of their smell. A character in Aristophanes' play *Thesmophoriazusae* explains that unfaithful women like herself 'eat garlic early in the morning after a night of wantonness, so that our husband, who has been keeping guard upon the city wall, may be reassured by the smell and suspect nothing'; presumably it would cover up the smell of wine and sex, or perhaps just keep the husband away. The latter reason was also why it was used in the ancient Greek harvest festival of Skira (or Skiraphoria), during which the women of Athens assembled, leaving their homes, and ate plenty of garlic. The idea was that they would abstain from sex in order to make the land more fertile.

Polybius' *Histories*, written in the second century BCE, tells of another trick to do with garlic. The Locrians of Greece, who had moved into the territory of the Sicels, managed to intimidate the Sicels into sharing their lands with them. The Sicels, fearful of the Locrians and unwilling to do battle, accepted this, since the Locrians had promised that 'they would be friendly and share the country with them, as long as they stood upon the ground they then stood upon, and kept heads upon their shoulders.' But unknown to the Sicels, the Locrians were doing the equivalent of keeping their fingers crossed behind their backs: they put earth inside their shoes and hid heads of garlic under their clothes and on their shoulders before they swore. Then they removed both, and soon afterwards banished the Sicels from the country.

Alexander the Great (356–321 BCE) supposedly introduced the shallot to his empire after discovering it in Palestine; it was said to come from Ashkelon (now in Israel), and this snippet of information has survived in the Latin binomial that was formerly given to the shallot, *Allium ascalonicum*. (This Latin name is now considered redundant and is no longer used, since shallots are interfertile with members of the *A. cepa* group. The 'true' shallot, or *A. oschaninii*, is a different plant.)

The Romans loved onions, and used them to flavour many dishes as well as taking them on their travels and introducing them to the lands of northern Europe. Although *cepa* is the Latin word for onion, the Romans called them *unionem* (from which our modern 'onion' derives) as well as *bulbus*. Columella, a Roman soldier turned farmer of the first century CE, gives a recipe for pickled onions:

> First dry the onions in the sun, then cool in the shade. Arrange it in a pot with thyme or marjoram strewn underneath, and after pouring in a liquid consisting of

The wild pink onion (*Allium trichocoleim* Bornm.) of Palestine, photographed by an American photographer in Jerusalem in 1942.

three parts vinegar and one part brine, put a bunch of marjoram on top . . . When they have absorbed the liquid, let the vessel be filled up with a similar liquid.[5]

There was a special variety of onion grown at Pompeii, for which Columella gives a recipe.

In a collection of Roman recipes written in the fourth or fifth century BCE and named after the famous glutton Marcus Gavius Apicius, onions, garlic and leeks are ubiquitous. They add crunch to salads and flavour sauces, form a bed for fish, or are cooked and eaten as stews.

Another Fish Dish with Onions
Clean any kind of fish and place it properly in a saucepan with shredded dry Ascalonian onions [shallots] or with any other kind of onions, the fish on top. Add stock and oil and cook. When done, put broiled bacon in the centre, give it a dash of vinegar, sprinkle with finely chopped savory and garnish with the onions.

But the real star of the allium family, for both Romans and Greeks, was the leek. So beloved was it that it gave its name in both Greek and Latin to the word *prasinos*, *prasinus*, 'green', sometimes called 'leek green', as distinct from pale green or *cloron*. The name 'chrysoprase', a type of green quartz, means 'the colour of leek juice'. The Greek word for a garden plot, *prasia*, also meant 'leek bed'. Leeks accompanied the Romans as they conquered other lands, since they were just too delicious to be left behind; establishing a leek bed must have been a necessary part of settling in to a new home. Leek seeds have been found in excavations of Roman sites in France, Britain and Germany, so it is likely to be the Romans whom the Welsh have to thank for introducing to them their national symbol.[6]

In this fragment of a Roman fresco panel of 100–150 CE, a meal is being prepared. A head of garlic awaits cooking on the left.

Apicius suggests boiling mature leeks in a mixture of water and oil with a pinch of salt, and then stewing them in oil and 'the best kind of broth'; they also feature in recipes involving other vegetables, and in one for a laxative.

Leeks were supposed to make the voice more brilliant, which is why the Emperor Nero (37–68 CE) was known as Porophagus, the leek-eater; of course, he may have been a glutton for them, but he may also have been trying to improve his oratory or his singing when he decided to eat nothing but leeks for two days each month.[7] Onions and leeks feature in nearly a hundred of Pliny the Elder's remedies, prescribed for health problems as varied as poor eyesight, dog bites, insomnia, venereal disease, toothache, dysentery and lumbago. Garlic, especially, also had medicinal uses – 61 of them, according to Pliny, who in his *Natural History* enthuses:

> The very smell of it drives away serpents and scorpions, and, according to what some persons say, it is a cure for wounds made by every kind of wild beast, whether taken with the drink or food, or applied topically . . . garlic draws

out the humours from fistulous sores, and employed with pitch, it will extract an arrow even from the wound.

He does, however, warn that 'The inconveniences which result from the use of it, are dimness of the sight and flatulency; and if taken in too large quantities, it does injury to the stomach, and creates thirst'; perhaps these are minor bothers compared with being shot by an arrow.

Hippocrates (*c.* 460–*c.* 370 BCE), the father of medicine, prescribed garlic as a diuretic and advised that it would help to ease the breath and heal wounds. But however loved it might have been as a medicine, it was forbidden to some monks and ascetics, because of the problem of smelly breath.[8]

China

The Confucian text the *Classic of Rites* (*Li ji*, perhaps 200 BCE) described ceremonies associated with important life events, such as marriages, sacrifices, mourning rites and feasts. Careful instructions were given on good conduct and the proper way to mark these events, as well as the behaviour of scholars and various other members of society. From this text we can see how alliums had already become an indispensable part of cuisine in what is today China. The *Classic of Rites* describes a dinner setting:

> The rules for bringing in the dishes for an entertainment are the following: The meat cooked on the bones is set on the left, and the sliced meat on the right; the rice is placed on the left of the parties on the mat, and the soup on their right; the minced and roasted meat are put outside (the chops and sliced meat), and the pickles and sauces

inside; the onions and steamed onions succeed to these, and the drink and syrups are on the right.

The text describes the use of onions and shallots in sacrifices; they were sliced and added to the brine in which pieces of meat were preserved before the whole was presented as an offering. It also details the practices of seasonal eating, and of matching different kinds of allium to the preparation of different meats:

> Mince was made in spring, with onions; in autumn, with the mustard plant. Sucking-pig was used in spring, with scallions; in autumn, with smartweed. With lard they used onions; with fat, chives.

Evidently onions played a large part in Chinese cuisine of the period, though Taoists of the fourth century forbade the use of 'five vegetables of strong odour', which included onions (some Buddhists still do not eat onions or garlic). They were supposed to be particularly detrimental to the lungs and to increase aggressiveness and sexual urges. In the Han Dynasty (206 BCE–220 CE) onions and garlic on red cords were hung from doorways to keep insects out.

South Central Asia

Various ancient Sanskrit texts describe the origins of garlic, which was regarded as a powerful medicine. The story goes that a group of wise men were wandering in the Himalayas, learning about the different plants that grew there and finding out their medicinal properties. One particular plant, with leaves as blue as sapphires and bulbs as white as the lotus flower, caught their eye. They took it to a sage to ask what it could be. He told them that it was garlic: a few drops of nectar had fallen from the heavens, and garlic had grown from these drops.

A fourth- or early fifth-century collection of writings now known as the Bower Manuscript, named after the British lieutenant who bought it from a local trader while he was tracking a fugitive through the Himalayas and across the Gobi Desert in 1890, gives a short history of the mythical origin of garlic and its medical uses, and celebrates it in 43 verses of poetry. In another variation of the story, it explains that the king of the demons drank the elixir of immortality, and that Lord Vishnu cut off his head as a punishment. The drops of blood became garlic when they fell to earth. It was said to cure all sorts of ills, from epilepsy to worms and rheumatism – although Brahmins are forbidden to eat it, because it originates from a body, that of the demon king. The manuscript, written in Sanskrit and Prakrit, includes a recommendation of a way to absorb the goodness of garlic if one has been forbidden it because of one's religion: one can simply keep a cow from eating grass for three days, and then feed her one part garlic stalks to two parts grass. Brahmins would be permitted to eat the curds and ghee made from her garlic-infused milk.

Korea

Garlic and green onions have been cultivated in Korea since the earliest times. There are records of garlic being culti-vated on the peninsula since the Three Kingdoms period (57 BCE–668 CE), and it was in fact the Koreans who introduced it to Japan.

Garlic is not only an integral part of much Korean cooking, but plays a part in the foundation myth of Gojoseon, an

Sculpture of garlic, South Korea. Daejeon in South Korea is also home to the Uiseong Garlic Museum.

ancient Korean kingdom that is said to have been founded in 2333 BCE. According to legend, the Lord of Heaven had a son, Hwanung, who descended to live on earth and found a holy city, Shinsi. A bear and a tiger prayed to Hwanung in the hope of becoming human. Hearing their prayers and taking pity on the pair, Hwanung gave them twenty cloves of garlic and a bundle of mugwort, and instructed them to stay in the cave in which they lived. They were to remain out of the sunlight and eat only the garlic and mugwort he had provided for a period of one hundred days. Thus would their prayers be answered. Sadly, the tiger was unable to keep to the vigil, but the bear followed the rules faithfully and after 21 days she was transformed into a woman called Ungnyeo. Eventually, after praying for a child, she was taken as a wife by Hwanung. Later she gave birth to Dangun Wanggeom, the legendary founder of the kingdom of Gojoseon, who was known as the 'grandson of heaven'.

2

The Medieval Onion

Well loved he garlic, onions, aye and leeks.
Geoffrey Chaucer, *The Canterbury Tales* (*c.* 1387–95)

Garlic had been introduced all over northern Europe by the
Romans, and after their mighty empire was finally defeated
by Germanic tribes, garlic still kept its place in European cuisine and elsewhere. The first major work of Rabbinic literature,
the Mishnah of *c.* 220 CE, states that Jews were known as 'the
garlic-eaters'. This may be a reference to the fact that the Roman
emperor Marcus Aurelius is supposed to have remarked on
how Jews smelled of garlic. (It may have been an allusion to
the racist idea that Jews had a particular stench, rather than
referring to their actual eating habits.) The Talmud suggested
that men should eat garlic on Friday nights in order to improve
their virility: it was supposed to increase semen production and
ardour, and Friday night was the time when Jewish women
would take their ritual baths as a precursor to lovemaking.
However, it's not clear how many Jews considered garlic an
integral part of their culture. The Jewish physician Maimonides
(1135–1205), for example, left any reference to garlic out of
his guidelines for eating. In any case, Jews were often depicted
with garlic in medieval illustrations.

In around the year 800 Charlemagne, whose empire spread from the north of Europe to the Mediterranean, enacted a charter in which he prescribed the 90 types of vegetable and fruit tree that should be grown in gardens around his empire; among them were onions, leeks, shallots, bunching (or Welsh) onions and garlic. Alliums were therefore well established in Europe, and were grown in the vegetable gardens of large estates such as monasteries.

The onion was one of the most popular vegetables in Europe during the Middle Ages. It is no coincidence that it is also easy to grow, high-yielding and simple to preserve.

Planting garlic, from the *Tacuinum sanitatis*, a medieval guide to health and well-being.

Encased in its own perfectly suitable packaging, and if kept dry and away from sunlight, the onion can stay fresh for up to six months: a particularly useful trait before the invention of refrigeration and air freighting. And unlike many vegetables or fruits, where a large plant may yield only a small amount of food, a large proportion of the plant can be eaten. Even the thinned-out young seedlings can be used, as spring onions. And, perhaps most important of all, the onion is reasonably tolerant of frost and cold conditions, so can be grown throughout northern Europe as well as in the south. We know of six kinds of allium regularly eaten in early medieval Britain: *cropleac* (which might be everlasting onion or chives), *garleac* (garlic), *porleac* (garden leek), *ynioleac* (onion), *hol-leac* and *brade-leac*.[1] In the Middle Ages food plants were divided into 'herbs', which grew above ground, and 'roots', which grew below. Thus onions, garlic and leeks were all considered herbs and were often used chopped as garnishes.

Of course, another reason why the onion was so popular in the Middle Ages was its versatility. It could be added to soups and stews or used to lend sweetness or depth of flavour to what otherwise might be an unexciting dish. Pottages, a common medieval dish a little like porridge, were made with boiled grain such as barley, sometimes with vegetables added; an onion in the cooking liquid would add fragrance and sweetness. Ordinary people would not have had ovens in their homes, but onions can be baked in the hot ashes of a fire, rather as one can bake a potato in its skin. Roasted onions, a sweet and aromatic treat, were therefore within reach of many people. Nearly everyone with a little land could, and did, grow them. Alliums of all sorts were so popular that even at this time, supply in Britain couldn't keep up with demand: onions, onion seed and garlic were all brought over from the Netherlands and Spain to be traded.[2]

William Langland's narrative poem *The Vision of Piers Plowman* (1360–87) gives us an impression of the mainstays of the English peasant's diet in medieval times:

All the poor people then their peascods fetched,
Beans and baked apples they brought in their laps,
Onions and chervil and many ripe cherries,
And proffered Piers this present wherewith to please
  Hunger.

Meat had they not; but they certainly had onions.

Onions had another advantage in poor people's food, too – their strength of flavour. At a time when poor people's meat was often only the 'umbles' of an animal – the liver, lungs, intestines and other offal – onions could improve the flavour, and perhaps even mask it; this may be why they were traditionally matched with liver, to make a dish that is still eaten to this day in Britain.[3] Indeed, the German *Buch von guter Spise* (Book of Good Food, 1354) suggests serving onions with liver in a stuffing for roast goose – although they accompany eggs and apples, not the sage that would be more common in Britain today.

In the Prologue to Chaucer's *The Canterbury Tales*, the Summoner, a corrupt official in the ecclesiastic court, is described as a loud and pungent individual, a drunkard with a red face encrusted with pimples:

With black and scabby brows and scanty beard;
He had a face that little children feared.
There was no mercury, sulphur, or litharge,
No borax, ceruse, tartar, could discharge,
Nor ointment that could cleanse enough, or bite,
To free him of his boils and pimples white,

Nor of the bosses resting on his cheeks.
Well loved he garlic, onions, aye and leeks,
And drinking of strong wine as red as blood.

Onions were said to be bad for the complexion, hence the rounded pustules on the Summoner's face. In Chaucer's description you can almost smell the blend of onion fumes and stale alcohol emanating from him (all of which underscores his corruption). Garlic was, after all, known as 'the stinking rose'.

Because of its ubiquity among all classes as a cheap and widely available food, the onion could be considered a vulgar vegetable. Perhaps this is why it is the subject of a rather rude tenth-century riddle in Old English recorded in the Exeter Book, an anthology of poetry and other literature.

I am a wondrous creature: to women a thing of joyful expectation, to close-lying companions serviceable. I harm no city-dweller excepting my slayer alone. My stem is erect and tall – I stand up in bed – and whiskery somewhere down below. Sometimes a countryman's quite comely daughter will venture, bumptious girl, to get a grip on me. She assaults my red self and seizes my head and clenches me in a cramped place. She will soon feel the effect of her encounter with me, this curl-locked woman who squeezes me. Her eye will be wet.

The French historian Bruno Laurioux argues that there was a hierarchy of foodstuffs in the medieval mind that was largely determined by how far off the ground they grew. The highest-ranking foods were fruits that grew on trees, and after them, fruits that grew on bushes. Slightly lower were foods that grew on stems, such as peas, and then those that grew from roots, like spinach. Roots themselves – carrots

An onion, coloured woodcut from Arnaldus de Villanova, *Ortus sanitatis* (1491).

and turnips – came next. Onions, shallots, garlic and leeks, as bulbs, were right at the bottom of the hierarchy – which made them the most humble vegetables possible, and suitable for any peasant. (Incidentally, meats were also subject to this hierarchy. Birds were ranked higher than pigs, for example.)

Onions and leeks were not just poor man's fare in the Middle Ages, however. Since the Church specified that many days of the year were to be fast days – Wednesdays, Fridays, some Saturdays, the days of Advent and Lent and certain other dates – it was important for the cooks of the aristocracy and high-ranking clergy to be able to provide tasty meatless food. *Le Menagier de Paris* (1393), which was written as a guide for a young housewife, suggests cooking onions up in a pot to make a stock in which peas could be cooked on 'fish days', rather than using bacon stock. And meatless foods had to be sophisticated in flavour and cooking technique to tempt the palates of the pious wealthy. *The Forme of Cury*, an English manuscript of about 1390 compiled by Richard II's cooks, recommends the classic combination of onions and cheese in a pie:

> Take and perboile oynouns & erbis & presse out þe water & hewe hem smale. Take grene chese & bray it in a morter, and temper it vp with ayren. Do þerto butter, saffroun & salt, & raisons corauns, & a litel sugur with powdour douce, & bake it in a trap, & serue it forth.

Saffron was terribly expensive in the Middle Ages, just as it is today, and sugar too was pricey before the time of cheap sugar made from sugar beet – though sweetness would also have come from the onions. This pie would certainly be fit to grace any table, whether or not meat dishes were also available.

The Old English *leac-tun* meant vegetable garden, and *leac-ward* meant gardener: so 'leek' really just means 'vegetable': a sign of their popularity. The white parts of leeks were preferred, as they were believed to be less dangerous to the health, and in medieval times most vegetables were pretty well-cooked – perhaps even overcooked by today's standards. Salads were eaten too, however.

Leeks were certainly the most eaten allium in Wales. They are one of only two vegetables mentioned in the laws of Hywel Dda, or Howell the Good (*c.* 880–950), who by the time of his death ruled over most of Wales (the other was cabbages).[4] A medieval Welsh medical text, 'Physicians of Myddfai', states that it is 'good for women who desire children to eat [leeks]'.[5]

Cambria; or, an Emblem of Wales, 1798, hand-coloured etching. Behind the allegorical figure of Wales, an infant holds up her crown, complete with leeks.

Henry William Bunbury, *Pistol Eating Fluellen's Leak* [sic], *'Henry V'*, c. 1811–15.

The leek, of course, is the symbol of Wales, and is worn on the feast day of St David, the patron saint of the country, which is on 1 March. Various legends attest to this; one (which is apocryphal) says that King Cadwaladr of Gwynedd ordered his soldiers to wear the vegetable on their helmets in a battle against the Saxons that took place in a leek field in the sixth century.

The custom was known in Shakespeare's day: in *Henry V*, set around two hundred years in the past, at the time of the Battle of Agincourt in 1415, the Welsh army captain Fluellen explains that he has been offended by Pistol, a fellow soldier. On seeing Fluellen wearing a leek in his cap on St David's Day, Pistol brings him bread and salt and advises him to eat the leek. Once the saint's day is past, Fluellen gets his revenge. Pistol is forced to eat the leek from Fluellen's cap or face four days of beatings: 'I beseech you heartily, scurvy, lousy knave, at my desires, and my requests, and my petitions, to eat, look

THE PHYSICIAN'S

RECEIPT

To cure a Welshman of a Fever, or to kill an English-
man with the same Medicine.

A GENTLEMAN of Wales coming fresh of the mountains to visit London, happened upon a change of air, to fall dangerously ill of a hectic fever. An English physician being immediately sent for, found his condition to be very dangerous, and presently ordered him such proper medicines as are usually administered in such cases, but all to no purpose; for the distemper proved so very rebellious that notwithstanding the doctor proceeded according to the best of his judgment, yet all thy physic he prescribed him, was wholly ineffectual, till at last the patient was reduced to so low a condition, that the doctor though a skilful man, quite despaired of his recovery, so told the nurse privately, that he had done the utmost according to the rules of art, and that all his visits and prescriptions for the future would be of little use to the patient, so that he would now give him up to the goodness of God and the care of herself, for he could not conceive it was in the power of physic to save his life, therefore advised her to deal gently by him, and deny him nothing that he could eat or drink, that the few moments he had to spend in this world might pass away under the less uneasiness; so took leave of the nurse and away he went.

No sooner had the doctor given the nurse this liberty, but as soon as his back was turned, she began to fondle her dying patient and begged of him to think of something or other that he thought he could eat or drink, and let it be what it would she would get it him presently; at last he lifted up his languishing eyes, and staring her full in the face, cried out as loud as he was able to speak, 'Toasted-Cheese.' With that she ran in all haste to the next chandler, notwithstanding she thought it strange food for a dying man in a fever, yet she resolved he should have it; and accordingly bought a pound of good old Cheshire, and cooked it so agreeable to her Welsh patient's tooth, that he eat it up every bit to the nurse's great astonishment. She then asked him what he thought he could drink? He told her then with a much stronger voice than before, 'A gallon of leek-pottage.' The nurse finding the toasted cheese agree so well with her patient ran immediately to the herb stall for a bunch of leeks, and brewed him up a gallon of Welsh candle presently, which, as soon as it was cool enough for his palate, he drank off, and then turning his face from the light composed himself to rest, and slept heartily till the next morning; and when he awaked was so extremely mended, that the nurse had great hopes of his recovery.

In the afternoon the doctor happening to come that way in his coach gave a look up at his chamber, expecting the dead signal, that is, the windows to be open, but finding them shut, stopped his coach and stepped up stairs to see how matters went, and coming into the chamber found the patient he had given over but the day before, to his great admiration getting out of bed.

The doctor was perfectly amazed at this unexpected sight, and enquired of the nurse what strange measures she had taken to recover him; who very readily told him what an unaccountable refreshment she had given him. 'Nurse,' says the doctor very gravely, smelling to the civet-box of his ebony cane, 'you have done very well; pray let him have more toasted cheese and more leek-porridge, and I will call again to-morrow and see how it agrees with him.'

The patient liked it so well that as often as they repeated it, he was willing to take it, till in a little time the Welshman was thoroughly recovered, upon which the nurse was well paid, and the physician had the reputation of a very wonderful cure.

In a little time after this miraculous success, the doctor happened to have an English patient exactly in the same condition, that by all the rules of art, by which he governed his practice, he could not administer one medicine that would abate the distemper; at last, calling to mind what a wonderful cure the nurse and he had so lately performed by toasted cheese and leek-porridge, not knowing but there might be some occult quality in one or the other more than physicians were acquainted with, he resolved to make trial of their virtues a second time, and accordingly directed the nurse to administer them to the patient, whom the doctor declared was absolutely past recovery by any other means.

The nurse thought it strange advice from a college physician, but however it being his directions, she was resolved to observe them, and accordingly provided a plentiful platefull of balsamatic Cheshire, toasted secundum artem, which with much ado she persuaded her patient to swallow after much kecking, and to take a hearty draught of leek pottage after it to help digestion. No sooner had the feeble patient forced down both his doses, but he turned his face to the wall, and instead of going to sleep, in less than a quarter of an hour he made his exit.

The doctor coming next day to enquire after the success of his new medicament, looking up for the old signal, found the windows wide open, by which he presently understood, without further enquiry, what condition his patient was in; so altering his course plucks out his pocket book and in it makes this memorandum:— 'Toasted cheese and leek pottage, a certain cure for a Welshman in a fever, but present death for an Englishman.' Probatum est.

Printed and sold by J. Pitts, 14. Great st. Andrew street, seven Dials,
Price Three Halfpence.

Broadsheet of 'The Physician's Receipt', a tale of a Welshman who is cured of a fever by eating toasted cheese and leek porridge, and an Englishman who dies on being given the same treatment, c. 1802–19.

you, this leek'. Pistol tries to get out of it by claiming that the smell makes him feel ill, but the injured Welshman cannot be dissuaded: 'I pray you,' says Fluellen, 'fall to: if you can mock a leek, you can eat a leek.' Even after he has eaten it, Pistol gets a stern talking-to about being disrespectful: 'Will you mock at an ancient tradition, begun upon an honourable respect, and worn as a memorable trophy of predeceased valour . . .?', asks another soldier:

> I have seen you gleeking and galling at this gentleman twice or thrice. You thought, because he could not speak English in the native garb, he could not therefore handle an English cudgel: you find it otherwise; and henceforth let a Welsh correction teach you a good English condition.

Wales still uses the leek as its national symbol: it appears on the Welsh pound coin and is the cap badge of the Welsh Guards, a regiment of the British Army. But Wales is not the only place in the United Kingdom to have a special relationship with the allium family. The classic Scottish dish of cock-a-leekie soup, a chicken soup with leeks, was invented in the medieval period – although at that time the recipe may also have included prunes, and the name probably came later, in the eighteenth century. Scotch broth, too, includes leeks and onions and is usually garnished with chopped green leek. And the vegetable is forever celebrated in the name of the Staffordshire town of Leek, which was granted a royal charter in 1207.

Medieval Medicine: The Humours

The ancient Greeks had outlined a theory of the human body that held sway throughout medieval Europe. The humoral theory stated that there were four basic 'humours' – sanguine, phlegmatic, choleric and melancholy. These were different temperaments that were also associated with certain bodily fluids. Good health resulted when these fluids were in balance, and certain foods could be eaten, or avoided, in order to rebalance the body. Recipe books from medieval times therefore read rather like prescriptions or medicinal textbooks, not just guides to good eating, and cooks in aristocratic households would be expected to keep an eye on the health implications of what they were serving up. The seasons and a person's age could affect what kinds of food were good for them, as could their lifestyle: a mostly sedentary aristocrat would need different food from a farm labourer, for example.

Leeks and onions were believed to be 'wet' and 'hot', and might therefore be a risky prospect for sanguine individuals, who were themselves warm and moist, since the vegetables would exacerbate these tendencies and throw the body out of balance. However, they would be ideal eating for melancholics, who were cold and dry. The seasons, too, had humoral properties that had to be considered when setting a menu. Autumn was cold and dry, so might be a good time to sample your baked leeks; but eating an onion soup in spring might exacerbate its humoral qualities to a dangerous extent, causing imbalance and ill-health. (Of course, in Europe onions are harvested in the late summer and autumn, so you would be likely to eat them at the right time of year in any case.)

If you were a sanguine individual, however, you didn't have to give up your favourite allium dishes: foods could be balanced by being combined with complementary ingredients. The smaller the parts they were minced or chopped into, the easier it was for two ingredients with the opposite qualities to neutralize each other. Sauces were therefore a great way of lessening the danger inherent in eating the wrong kind of food, which may be one reason why they were so popular. Sauces were an important element of aristocratic cuisine, and royal households might have their own sawsery, a special office in the kitchen manned by a professional saucier. Garlic was a particularly popular ingredient in such sauces. *Le Viandier*, a French recipe collection dating from around 1300, lists several different recipes for garlic sauce. For white cameline garlic sauce, one simply crushed garlic and steeped it in verjuice, thickening it with bread. After eating garlic, one could eat herbs or drink vinegar in order to freshen the breath.

Other cooking techniques could also mitigate any potential health problems: onions were often fried to remove their dangerous moisture, for example.[6] And spices, a great feature of the medieval kitchen, were generally hot and dry, so would be ideal additions that would balance out an onion dish.

3
Travel, Trade and Folklore

Whoever rubs himself with garlic will not smell of cloves.

French proverb

Even in the Elizabethan period, several foreign onion varieties were known; they were moved and traded all over Europe in an early instance of food miles, perhaps because onions are easy to store and pack. The English herbalist and botanist John Parkinson (1567–1650), who was later apothecary to James I and kept a famous botanical garden in the centre of London at Long Acre, not far from today's Trafalgar Square, wrote in a treatise on the cultivation of plants: 'The long kinde wee call St Omers Onions, and corruptly among the vulgar, St Thomas Onions.' Saint-Omer is a town in northwestern France, around 30 miles from the English Channel. The gardener and diarist John Evelyn (1620–1706), in *Acetaria: A Discourse of Sallets* (yes, a whole book about salads), wrote that the best onions came from Spain, and the poet John Skelton also wrote in 1522 of 'the Spaniardes' onyons'. Martin Lister mentioned in his *Journey to Paris* (1699) some varieties eaten by the French: 'large Red Onions . . . And the long and sweet white Onion of Languedoc'.

Europeans also took their favourite vegetables with them as seed when colonizing new countries. The first printed

41 Vende Agli e Cipolle.

Simon Guillain after Annibale Carracci, vendor of garlic and onions,
Bologna, *c.* 1646.

Allium acuminatum, an indigenous North American variety also known as Hooker's onion or the tapertip onion.

mention of onions in the New World was by one William Wood, in his *New Englands Prospect*, which in the words of his subtitle was 'a true, lively and experimentall description of that part of America, commonly called New England: discovering the state of that Countrie, both as it stands to our new-come English Planters, and to the old Native Inhabitants'.[1] It was published in London in 1634, just five years after Wood had first emigrated to the New World (and fourteen after the voyage of the *Mayflower*). In it, he mentioned that onions were easily to be cultivated in the kitchen gardens of Massachusetts at that time, presumably from seed the settlers had brought with them from Europe. Evidently onions were considered a staple.

There were indigenous alliums on the American continent, too: meadow leeks, also known as rose leeks or Canada garlic, were eaten by Native Americans. The explorer and

Jesuit missionary Jacques Marquette, who founded the first colony in Michigan, ate these in 1673 on his journey up the Mississippi to what is now Chicago. The name of the city derives from *shika-kwaa*, a Native American term meaning 'place of the wild garlic'. Even today, the city is sometimes known as the Big Onion to New York's Big Apple. Onions and garlic were also taken by European colonists to settlements in South and Central America. It is said that Columbus took the cultivated onion to Hispaniola, now Haiti and the Dominican Republic, in 1492.

But the story of onions and garlic is not confined to the Western world. It also featured in another great early modern cookery tradition: that of the Mughal empire. Dopiaza (from the Persian for '(having) two onions') is a regional dish of the Hyderabadi region. It is said that it was developed by the courtier Mullah Do Piaza (quite a coincidence, surely?) at the court of the great emperor Akbar (1542–1605). The mullah, who may or may not be fictional, was supposedly a famous wit and is depicted in folk tales as outsmarting both the emperor and other courtiers. To make dopiaza, fry a quantity of sliced onions with spices before adding meat, garlic and ginger; after the dish is cooked, add yet more sliced, spiced, caramelized onions as a garnish (hence the name, 'onions twice'). 'Curries' around the world as we know them today – Indian-inspired (though inauthentic) dishes of meat or vegetables cooked in a spicy sauce – usually feature onions and garlic, which are often chopped finely or crushed to a paste with spices or ginger before being added to the pot. The British helped to spread this version of Indian cuisine wherever they went, and it's no surprise that the resulting dishes often included vegetables that were readily available and eaten by everyone in Britain. The standard dishes found in every local Indian takeaway in the UK – bhuna, jalfrezi,

The legendary Mullah Do Piaza riding a horse in an 18th-century Indian manuscript from Hyderabad.

dopiaza, rogan josh, biryani – are also heavily flavoured with onion and garlic.

This is not to say that all authentic Indian food contains alliums. Far from it. The Ayurveda, the system of traditional Indian medicine which dates back to the early first millennium CE, dictates that some castes (Brahmins, the scholarly class, and Vaishyas) should not eat onions and garlic. This is because they are believed to increase passion and anger and be detrimental to meditation. They do have medicinal uses, however:

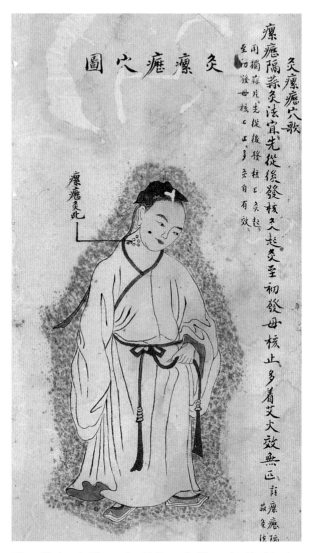

灸瘰癧穴歌

圖穴癧瘰灸

瘰癧隔蒜灸法寅先從後發核久起灸至初發毋核止多著艾火效無匹諸瘰癧隔

用獨蒜片先從後發核上灸起至初後核上正灸灸自有效

瘰癧灸此

Zhang Youheng's *Chuanwu ling ji lu* (Record of Sovereign Teachings), a Chinese medical treatise of 1869. This illustration demonstrates how to treat scrofula with garlic in a process called moxibustion, which involves burning mugwort and other herbs above acupuncture points.

one might eat garlic to help with impotence or other health problems.

Members of the Swaminarayan sect do not eat onions or garlic either, since the ancient scripture the Vachanamrut advises against them. Neither do Kashmiri pandits. Jainism, one of the oldest world religions (it may date back around 3,000 years), also forbids the eating of alliums. Unlike the proscriptions (or warnings) in the Hindu texts, this is not only because the vegetables themselves are believed to have a detrimental effect on those who eat them, but because harvesting them may cause harm to small organisms. Jainism is a religion based on the principle of non-violence (*ahimsa*), and all Jains are vegetarian; many are vegan. Root vegetables are considered *ananthkay*, which means that they contain many lives. Pulling them up may harm small insects and organisms that live in the soil, as well as killing the plant itself.

It has been speculated that onions are used so much in Indian food because of their antibiotic and antimicrobial effect (on which more later), like the spices that accompany them. In Europe, too, in the early modern period, food was still seen as medicinal, just as it had been in the medieval period, and the theory of the humours was still influential. Evelyn's *Acetaria*, published in 1699, repeated some of the old chestnuts of the Middle Ages:

> we own them [onions] in *Sallet*, not so hot as *Garlick*, nor at all so rank: Boil'd, they give a kindly relish; raise Appetite, corroborate the Stomach, cut Phlegm, and profit the *Asthmatical*: But eaten in excess, are said to offend the Head and Eyes, unless *Edulcorated* [cleansed] with a gentle maceration.

Leeks, too, were commended: they were thought

This Ottoman manuscript from 1717 depicts staples: rice, spinach, wild alliums and camel's thorn.

hot, and of Vertue Prolifick, since *Latona*, the Mother of *Apollo*, long'd after them: The *Welch*, who eat them much, are observ'd to be very fruitful: They are also friendly to the Lungs and Stomach . . . a few therefore of the slender and green *Summities*, a little shred, do not amiss in Composition.

Evelyn was a little more cautious about garlic, however, seeming incredulous that the hot-blooded Spaniards and Italians could stomach it to the extent they did, given that it was 'dry

'Buy my Four Ropes of Hard Onyons', one of a bound series of etchings by Marcellus Laroon of *The Cryes of City of London Drawne after the Life*, 1688.

James Gillray, *French Liberty, British Slavery*, 1792. This Revolution-era print shows the newly emancipated French in poverty living on raw onions, while the English, under their king, enjoy roast beef.

towards Excess'. Evidently he doubted their belief that it was 'a Charm against all Infection and Poyson (by which it has obtain'd the Name of the *Country-man's Theriacle* [antidote])'. You wouldn't catch Evelyn adding it to his food:

> We absolutely forbid it entrance into our *Salleting*, by reason of its intolerable Rankness, and which made it so detested of old, that the eating of it was (as we read) part of the Punishment for such as had committed the horrid'st Crimes. To be sure, 'tis not for Ladies Palats, nor those who court them, farther than to permit a light touch on the Dish, with a *Clove* thereof.

This may be the period in which we start to see a split between the nations of northern and western Europe, which preferred the more retiring onions, and those of southern and eastern Europe, which loved the more powerful garlic. Certainly garlic appears to have become less popular in Britain at this time, and it was not a favourite of the new settlers in America. Garlic's pungency was seen as positive in some parts of Europe, however; Henri III of Navarre (1553–1610), who became Henri IV of France, was baptised in the traditional ritual of Navarre and Béarn: with a spoonful of wine and a garlic clove touched to his lips.

Of course, one of the most famous French dishes – to Britons and Americans, at least – is the classic French onion soup, made with caramelized onions simmered in beef broth and topped with a round of crusty, toasted bread covered in melted Gruyère cheese. This warming and savoury soup dates from around the sixteenth century, but is said to have been popularized by Stanisław I (1677–1766), king of Poland and duke of Lorraine. Stanisław was visiting his daughter Marie Leszczyńska, the queen of France, who was married to Louis XV. The story goes that on his journey to the French court, Stanisław stopped at an inn one night in Châlons and asked

Delicious but messy: French onion soup.

Church of the Transfiguration, Kizhi island, Russia, built in 1714. Onion domes resemble onions, but are actually thought to symbolize candle flames.

for some food. Unfortunately, all the inn had available for him and his men was some humble onion soup, but the king was so taken with the delicious broth that he brought the recipe with him to the French court, where it became popular. Apocryphal or no, it's certainly a good story, especially as it raises the image of the bewigged and jewelled Louis XV and his equally dandified courtiers trying to eat a soup that is notoriously difficult to consume politely, what with the strings of caramelized onion, crumbs and melted cheese.

Stanisław may also have been familiar with pickled onions, which are often eaten in Eastern Europe, where fermentation is a popular method of food preservation. They were said to be good for epilepsy. Moving further east, Russia has the most famous onion-inspired art in the world: the onion domes, which appeared during the reign of Ivan the Terrible in the sixteenth century. These onion-shaped domes were a feature of nearly every church built towards the end of the nineteenth century. Some of the most famous of these domes appear on St Basil's Cathedral in Moscow, but they can also be found in some Baroque Catholic churches in southern Germany, Austria and the Czech Republic, and in the Mughal architecture of India and in Iran.

Folklore and Magic

There was much European folklore surrounding the allium family, too, some of which survived until the Victorian period, or even later. The Renaissance Italian chef Bartolomeo Scappi mentioned in his cookery book *Opera* that some people added garlic to dishes of foraged mushrooms in order to draw out and absorb any poisons from improperly identified specimens. A similar myth was recorded in *The Times* as late as 1825:

> To try the quality of field mushrooms – Take an onion, and strip the outer skin, and boil it with them: if it remains white, they are good; but if it becomes blue or black, there are certainly dangerous ones among them.

You could try to cure baldness by rubbing onion juice on your head, as John Evelyn had recommended in his *Acetaria*. In Ireland you could use an onion poultice to attempt to cure a cough or cold, or, since it was supposed to be good for the chest, put wild garlic in your socks. This one actually has a scientific basis: the pungency of onions comes from a chemical

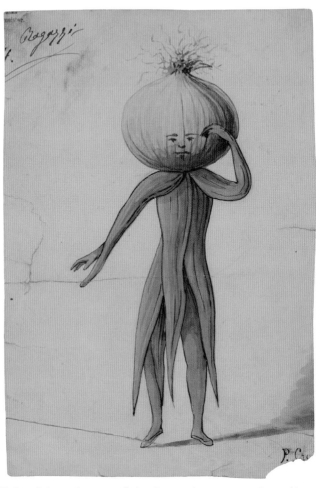

P. Croce's late 19th-century design for an onion costume to be used in
the Italian ballet *Amor*, choreographed by Luigi Manzotti and with music
by Romualdo Marenco. The ballet featured 200 dancers and 250 extras.

called allicin, which can be absorbed through the skin. If you put garlic in your socks you will indeed end up with garlic breath; which, to someone with a cold, might make you feel as though your airways are being cleared a little.[2]

It was said that dreaming about peeling onions foretold domestic problems or sickness, while dreaming about eating onions meant that you would find something valuable.[3] In Britain in the seventeenth century, placing a raw onion in a dish in a room containing a sick person was supposed to keep visitors safe by absorbing all the illness. This tradition was reported as late as the nineteenth century. On a similar theme, it was believed in some parts of Britain that if you buried onion peelings outside your house, they would draw out any fever from it. You could use them to predict bad weather, too: one traditional British rhyme states:

Onion skins very thin,
Mild winter coming in;
Onion skins thick and tough,
Coming winter cold and rough.

A rather charming custom was recorded in the fortune-telling chapbook *Mother Bunch's Closet Newly Broke Open* (first published in 1685): peel a St Thomas's onion, lay it on a clean handkerchief under your pillow and say the following rhyme:

Good St Thomas, do me right
Send me my true love tonight
That I may see him in the face
And in my arms may him embrace.

'Then in thy first sleep thou shalt dream of him that shall be thy husband', the book confirms – if the smell of the onion didn't keep you awake, that is. In the days before the Magic 8-ball, you had to predict your future with whatever was close at hand. A version of this custom was still taking place in 1871, when it was reported on in the British periodical *Notes and Queries*: girls would use onions on St Thomas's Eve (20 December) to predict their future. They would stick nine pins into a large red onion, and give the middle pin the name of the man they wished to marry. While doing this, they would recite a longer version of the rhyme, and would hope to dream of him that night.[4]

It had long been thought that garlic had some sort of magical powers to keep off evil, and in fact it was used by Crusaders to guard against illness and demons. One of the most famous folklore myths around garlic in the traditions of Eastern Europe and the Balkans is that it protects against vampires. The vampire as we know it today, a bloodsucking revenant who preys on humans, is descended from the mythological beings of Eastern Europe. The Slavs had long had a tale that unclean spirits could inhabit dead and decomposing bodies that had not been buried according to the proper rites, and that they might suck the blood of livestock and humans. Various agents have been put forward as possible apotropaics – wild rose and hawthorn twigs, mustard seeds, holy water and crucifixes – but many people in the West would go to garlic first if stalked by one of the undead.

This is no doubt because it is used repeatedly in one of the most famous vampire legends of all: Bram Stoker's *Dracula* (1897), which forms the basis of today's Western conception of vampires (one might even say that Stoker invented the modern vampire). In the book, Transylvanian villagers fill the food of the travellers with extra garlic and present them with garlic flowers. The vampire hunter Professor Van Helsing also attempts to protect Lucy Westenra against Count Dracula using garlic flowers:

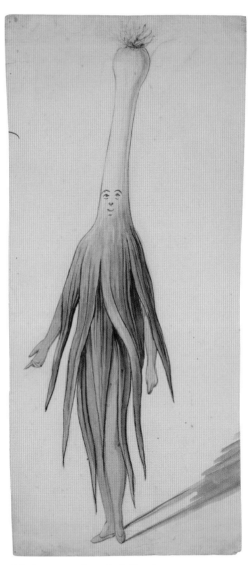

A leek costume from the ballet *Amor*.

First he fastened up the windows and latched them securely; next, taking a handful of the flowers, he rubbed them all over the sashes, as though to ensure that every whiff of air that might get in would be laden with the garlic smell. Then with the wisp he rubbed all over the jamb of the door, above, below, and at each side, and round the fireplace in the same way. It all seemed grotesque to me, and presently I said: –

'Well, Professor, I know you always have a reason for what you do, but this certainly puzzles me. It is well we have no sceptic here, or he would say that you were working some spell to keep out an evil spirit.'

'Perhaps I am!' he answered quietly as he began to make the wreath which Lucy was to wear round her neck.

We then waited whilst Lucy made her toilet for the night, and when she was in bed he came and himself fixed the wreath of garlic round her neck.

The comforted Lucy reports in her diary, 'I never liked garlic before, but to-night it is delightful! There is peace in its smell.' But all is in vain, since Lucy's mother, checking on her daughter during the night, thinks that the heavy smell of the flowers will make Lucy ill and takes them away, opening the window to air the room. Of course, the Count makes his way in to bite Lucy. As she gradually transforms into a vampire and dies, Dr Seward writes: 'It was certainly odd that whenever she got into that lethargic state, with the stertorous breathing, she put the flowers from her; but that when she waked she clutched them close.' In other words, when she is turning into a vampire, she hates the garlic, but her true, 'human' self sees the flowers as the protection that they are. As she becomes worse, they seem to bother her more and she tears them from her throat; when she dies soon afterwards, her coffin is filled with them. But they're not powerful enough to prevent her from rising as one of the Undead, and when Harker and Van Helsing finally cut Lucy's head off and drive a stake through her body so that she may rest, they fill her mouth with garlic.

It is notable that Van Helsing uses garlic flowers rather than cloves of garlic, which are much more common in modern versions of the vampire myth. Perhaps this can partly be put down to the fact that it would be easier for modern viewers to recognize cloves of garlic than garlic flowers on-screen; or perhaps it's simply that those wishing to protect themselves from vampires these days find the readily available and longer-lasting cloves of garlic more convenient.

In the comedy *The Fearless Vampire Killers; or, Pardon Me, but your Teeth are in my Neck* (dir. Roman Polanski, 1967), vampire hunter Professor Ambrosius is tipped off to the presence of a vampire's castle nearby when he stays at an inn liberally festooned with plaits of garlic bulbs. But modern interpretations of the vampire story on film often feel the need to explain that garlic doesn't work – perhaps because killing with a stake or silver bullet is a more stylish and dramatic visual image. In the classic 1980s teen vampire film *The Lost Boys* (dir. Joel Schumacher), the idea that garlic might protect against the undead is treated as a running joke. Various characters attempt to protect themselves with garlic, only to be informed, 'Garlic don't work, boys!' It's not even mentioned in the *Twilight* series, although *True Blood*'s Bill does find garlic 'unpleasant' and mildly irritating.

But why was garlic identified by Stoker as protecting against vampires in the first place? My suspicion is that it's tied up in Victorian ideas about the spread of disease. Before the advent of germ theory it was commonly thought that illnesses were spread by 'miasmas', or bad airs (of which Victorian Britain had plenty, including the famous London 'pea souper' fogs, which certainly were bad for the lungs). If pungent smells like that of garlic could overpower and neutralize the lurking diseases in the air, absorbing their miasmas, perhaps they could also fight off more supernatural predators.

Another theory about why garlic is thought to protect against vampires is that it's commonly believed to repel mosquitoes. If it can put off one bloodsucker, it can defend you from a bigger one, the argument goes. A Norwegian study in 1994 actually attempted to show whether garlic was indeed a good remedy against bloodsuckers. Leeches were presented with a choice of human hands to feed on: one garlic-smeared, and one not. The leeches actually seemed to prefer the garlicky hands, and so the scientists concluded that garlic might be attractive to vampires rather than a deterrent. Still, a leech and a vampire are very different things. And when a rumour went round in 2012 that the famous vampire Sava Savanović had risen and was terrorizing the villagers of Zarožje in Serbia, garlic sales in the region went through the roof.[5]

Besides the power to fight off vampires, the allium family is ascribed other useful qualities, too. In 1828 *The Times* recorded that a German horticultural writer recommended planting a large onion next to a rose bush, which he claimed would strengthen the smell of the roses; poking a little fun at him, the paper commented: 'Perhaps the German might prefer the smell of an onion to that of a rose.'

4
The Onion Improves

The onion is the truffle of the poor.
Jean Anthelme Brillat-Savarin

Great strides were made in farming in the eighteenth and nineteenth centuries. In Britain an agricultural revolution had occurred from around 1750, and as the population rose – from around 5.7 million to around 16.6 million in 1850 – food production rose with it. There were new techniques to increase productivity, such as crop rotation; land that had previously been unusable for arable farming, including the wetlands of East Anglia, was reclaimed through drainage or through clearing woodland; and new tools were invented, from seed drills to the first tractors, cutting down on the amount of manual labour required and improving efficiency.

Farming was becoming scientific, as farmers' manuals from the period reveal. The idea was that selective breeding would create better species of edible animals and plants that would have certain desirable characteristics, such as being resistant to pests or taking less time to grow. Yields were also improved by new, scientific methods of getting nitrogen into the soil. Farmers had previously done this by using animal manure, but in the Victorian era chemical fertilizers were

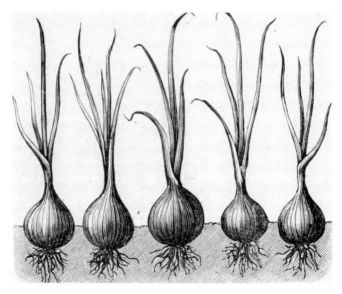

Onion row, from T. Greiner's manual *The New Onion Culture* (1891). The author states that 'Nothing short of hail and flood could prevent a good profit in this new onion culture, if managed with ordinary intelligence.'

available, as well as the less newfangled techniques of growing nitrogen-fixing plants such as clover (which are known as 'green manure') to improve the soil.

Gentlemen horticulturists began to interest themselves in the breeding of vegetables and plants, as well as flowers, with the aim of improving efficiency and yields. In 1804 the Horticultural Society of London was set up with the aim of improving horticultural practice by collecting and sharing information on it; its founders were John Wedgwood, son of the potter Josiah Wedgwood, and the great botanist and naturalist Sir Joseph Banks. Banks had accompanied Captain Cook on his first voyage and had introduced many plants to the West, including acacia, eucalyptus and mimosa, as well as *Banksia*, the genus named after him. In the late 1820s the

Society began to hold floral fetes, where members could display their new discoveries and the results of their experiments with hybridization. When the Society was granted a royal charter by Prince Albert in 1861, resulting in it being renamed the *Royal* Horticultural Society (RHS), these fetes became larger affairs, and led to the annual Show, which still takes place today. It remains a venue for promoting exciting new varieties of plants, with the hope of winning a coveted prize.

The new scientific approach to farming and breeding meant that a huge number of varieties of onion were developed that might be easier or quicker to grow, larger, tastier, longer-keeping or more disease-resistant than their ancestors. Consumer choice widened as transport networks improved and goods could be shipped quickly to all parts of the country – or even the world – before they spoiled. As a result the marketplace even for fairly humble items became more competitive. Improved breeds gave their growers the edge in the market. By 1883, Pierre Vilmorin's *Les Plantes potagères* (Kitchen Garden Plants) could list sixty varieties of onion sorted into seven categories – 'flat, flattened, disk-form,

Advertisement from H. W. Buckbee's plant and seed guide, 1907. The advantages of globe-shaped onions are listed at the bottom-right corner: attractiveness, economy of use, high market prices and increased profitability.

spherical, spherical-flattened, pear-shaped, or long' – though these distinctions have been superseded by today's technical terms to describe the different shapes of onion bulbs: 'globe, flattened globe, high globe, spindle, Spanish, flat, thick-flat, granex, and top-shaped'.[1] At the RHS fair in 1887 new breeds were displayed, including the prizewinning 'cocoa-nut'. *The Times* reported that it was 'admirably shaped, the poetry of onions', and that, when 'grown on English soil, [it] approximates in mildness of flavour to the onion crops of Spain'.[2]

One famous British venue at which onions were sold in the Victorian era was the Birmingham Onion Fair. Sometimes called the Michaelmas fair, since it was held on the last Thursday of September, it was at once an autumn festival and a bustling market. The *Illustrated London News* claimed that 'Nowhere can such large quantities be seen or of finer quality, than in the special Fair at Birmingham.'[3] The journalist James Greenwood visited the fair in 1874:

> You may smell them long before you reach the Bull Ring, which is the place where the fair is held. They give a pungency to the air, and you can taste them on the lips, as salt of the sea may be tasted before the watery waste is yet in sight. But this mild foretaste by no means prepares you for the spectacle that greets the visual organs, when from the High Street you look down the hill at the foot of which is St Martin's Church. There is a square paved space as large, say, as Clerkenwell Green, piled, heaped, stacked in blocks of onions, large as four-roomed houses. Onions in enormous crates, such as crockery arrives in from the Potteries, onions in hogsheads, onions in sacks, in bags like hop-pockets, in ropes or 'reeves,' loose in waggons that three horses draw; onions of all sizes and all qualities – 'brown shells,' 'crimsons,' 'whites,' 'big

Birmingham Onion Fair, from the *Illustrated London News*, 1872.

'uns,' and 'picklers.' Onions block the roadway and brim over on the pavement, and hang in bulky festoons about the railings that surround the statue of Lord Nelson, who is so exposed to the mounds and shoals that one might almost imagine the sourness of his iron visage was due to his dislike for the odour of the chief ingredient of goose-stuffing, and that he would be thankful could he but raise a handkerchief to his heroic nose and shut out the fragrance.[4]

Breeders also showed off their new creations in seed catalogues, which trumpeted the virtues of their new products in text bursting with excited adjectives and accompanied by bright illustrations. The marketing of these new varieties was slick and attractive. William Henry Maule's 'Prizetaker' was advertised in the Philadelphia-based company's catalogue for 1892 as 'the largest and best of all . . . average weight 2 lb each'. The cover boasted that there was 'No demand for other onions when Prizetakers are offered for sale', and that

Maule's 'Prizetaker', from the company's seed catalogue of 1891.

'Prizetakers have sold frequently for four times the price obtained for Wethersfield or Danvers.' But the catalogue cover of the John A. Salzer Seed Co. of Wisconsin in the spring of 1899 fought back for the Wethersfield, arguing that the company's new, improved variety was 'unquestionably the greatest onion on earth! . . . a vigorous grower, fine grained, long keeping onion – prodigally prolific, 1,213 bushels per acre – and all of the rarest quality'.

Another result of the interest in breeding was the development of non-edible alliums as decorative flowers, although they were not deployed widely in gardens – and certainly not in the house – until varieties had been developed that did not have quite so pungent a smell. Today they are among the most spectacular garden bulbs you can buy, with their distinctive large spherical heads made up of small star-shaped flowers. Several hundred varieties are available, and they can be up to 5 feet (1.5 m) tall, in colours ranging from purple and white to yellow and pink. Most ornamental varieties are produced in the Netherlands, including the popular 'Star of Persia', 'Globemaster' and 'Purple Sensation'. Descriptions of them in today's seed catalogues are no less enthusiastic than the ones of edible varieties more than a hundred years ago: *Allium album*, according to the website of British seed company Mr Fothergills, has

> Delicate panicles of white pendulous flowers produced on strong stems, accented by mid-green, strap-like leaves.
>
> It's great these majestic perennials are back in vogue – thanks to trend-setting designers who cannot get enough of them! Trouble-free and easy to grow, they make a statement in any border.

Yet despite all these improvements in growing and breeding, in the Victorian age the onion was still peasant's food in Britain. In its description of the Birmingham Fair, the *Illustrated London News* explained: 'The dealers and customers at this Fair are mostly the country folk of Warwickshire, with a few tradesmen of the town and some of the workmen's wives, for the onion gives a palatable relish to a poor man's dinner or supper.'[5] In *Oliver Twist* (1838) Charles Dickens describes the food served in the workhouse: 'three meals of thin gruel a-day, with an onion twice a-week, and half a roll on Sundays'. The inmates didn't even eat bread regularly, but onions were available. It must have been the only vitamin C they got.

The French chef Alexis Soyer, perhaps the most famous chef in Victorian England, was known as a cook for the highest in the land, but also set up soup kitchens during the Irish Famine and wrote several cookbooks of economical and nutritious recipes that the poor could follow. Many featured onions as flavouring for stocks or sauces, or to pad out stews of vegetables and the cheaper cuts of meat. His 'Soup for the Poor' of 1847, which he served at the soup kitchens, was bulked out with onions:

Alexis Soyer's Soup for the Poor
12½ lbs leg of beef
100 gallons of water
6¼ lbs drippings
100 onions and other vegetables
25 lbs each of flour (seconds) and pearl barley
1½ lbs brown sugar
9 lbs salt

Soyer claimed that a bowl of this a day, plus a biscuit, would be sufficient to nourish a person – although *Punch* quipped that rather than 'Soup for the Poor' it should be named 'Poor Soup'.

Picturesque poverty: John Singer Sargent, *Venetian Onion Seller*, 1882.

Léon Bonvin, *Cook with Red Apron*, 1862. This French watercolour depicts a simple scene in which the cook prepares commonplace vegetables: leeks, turnips, lettuce and carrots.

The English social researcher Henry Mayhew, in his *London Labour and the London Poor* (1851), reported that even the lowest of the low ate onions. This magisterial book of social research contains thousands of interviews with the working people of London, from street entertainers to prostitutes and mudlarks, who searched for sellable items in the mud of the banks of the Thames. He confirmed that 'The greatest sum of money expended by the poor upon any vegetable (after potatoes) is spent upon onions – 99,900*l.* being annually devoted to the purchase of that article', adding that a piece of bread and an onion was 'to the English labourer what bread and an apple or a bunch of grapes is to the French peasant – often his dinner'. He also described the poor onion-sellers of London, many of whom were Irish. 'Onion selling can be started on a small amount of capital', he explained, and quoted one Irish lady:

I'll tell you the thruth – we does best on ing-uns [onions] . . . The three of us now makes 1*s.* and sometimes 1*s.* 6*d.* a day, and that's grand doin's. We may sill [sell] bechuxt [between] us from two to three dozin ropes a day.

Even then, though, complaints were made about foreign street traders who undercut their competitors' prices, and one costermonger expressed a fear that this meant that he would soon no longer earn a living wage.

That Victorian housewife par excellence Mrs Beeton wasn't fond of garlic, but used onions liberally in sauces, soups and stews, as well as serving them up baked as a side dish (which, she reports, would come in at the thrifty sum of tuppence a head). She suggests the handy time-saving tip of caramelizing onions with water, sugar and vinegar and bottling the resultant elixir for use in gravy. In her *Book of Household Management*, she outlines the onion's properties, with just a little bit of caution:

> Of all the species of allium, the onion has the volatile principle in the greatest degree; and hence it is impossible to separate the scales of the root without the eyes being affected. The juice is sensibly acid, and is capable of being, by fermentation, converted into vinegar, and, mixed with water or the dregs of beer, yields, by distillation, an alcoholic liquor. Although used as a common esculent, onions are not suited to all stomachs; there are some who cannot eat them either fried or roasted, whilst others prefer them boiled, which is the best way of using them, as, by the process they then undergo, they are deprived of their essential oil. The pulp of roasted onions, with oil, forms an excellent anodyne and emollient poultice to suppurating tumours.

One can indeed make onion wine, although homebrew Internet forums report that it is best used as a marinade for chicken or fish, rather than a 'drinking wine' – a nice distinction. On their use to poultice suppurating tumours, I happily have nothing to report.

In France, too, onions were eaten by the poor. In 1871 it was suffering from the losses of the Franco-Prussian War, and the British National Society for Aid to the Sick and Wounded in War sent over a questionnaire, asking French farmers what they needed in order to survive. The answer was seed, and the Society collected 41,955*l.* 2*s.* 2*d.*, enough to pay for 1,000 quarter-pounds of onion seed to be sent to the Département de l'Aisne, as well as 1,000 quarter-pecks of turnip seed and 1,000 2-lb packets of carrot seed.[6]

Many of the French Impressionists eschewed the city to work in the countryside of France, particularly Provence. There they worked on still-lifes and other paintings that seem to sum up a simple, back-to-basics life in the French countryside. Paul Cézanne's *Still-life with Onions and Bottle* (1896–8), with its humble subject-matter, is an experiment in depicting different forms and textures. Renoir, too, used onions as a still-life study. And the Dutch painter Vincent Van Gogh also depicted onions many times in his paintings, from *Still-life with Red Cabbages and Onions* (1887) to *Still-life with Ginger Jar and Onions* (1885).

In America, too, onions were cheap and ubiquitous, although garlic does not seem to have been popular. The first American cookbook, *American Cookery* by Amelia Simmons, published in 1796, had recommended how to choose onions – 'the high red, round hard onions are the best' – as

Paul Cézanne, *Still-life with Onions and Bottle*, 1896–8.

Pierre-Auguste Renoir, *Onions*, 1881.

well as featuring them in recipes for wildfowl and waterfowl,
and fat pork cooked with Madeira (an odd mix of a cheap
meat with an expensive imported wine; perhaps it added a
tinge of luxury to an otherwise monotonous diet). When the
commanding general (and later president) Ulysses S. Grant
sent an urgent cable during the Civil War saying 'I will not
move my army without onions', he was indicating how very
dire the food situation had become for the soldiers. Fannie
Merritt Farmer, in the third edition of her *Boston Cooking-school
Cook Book* (1918), used them in all sorts of dishes, declaring
them 'wholesome' and to contain 'considerable nutriment';
in addition, she reports that 'the common garden onion is
available throughout the year', and recommends the more
'delicate' Bermuda or Spanish types that can be found in the
late spring. After giving a recipe for leeks on toast – 'Wash
and trim leeks, cook in boiling salted water until soft, and
drain. Arrange on pieces of buttered toast and pour over
melted butter, seasoned with salt and pepper' – she crisply
sums up the limited function of other members of the allium

family: 'Shallot, garlic, and chive are used, to some extent, in making salads.'

Travelling

Before the opening up of Japan in the Meiji period (1868–1912), the country guarded its borders and its culture fiercely. Foreigners did not have the right to travel freely within Japan or to make contact with locals, and Japanese people were forbidden to leave the country. It's no surprise, then, that the Central Asian/European variety *A. cepa* did not become a common ingredient in Japan until the nineteenth century. Until that time, the alliums eaten in Japan were mostly the bunching onion, *A. fistulosum*, known as *negi*, which is still the most popular vegetable in the country. But when Westerners began to trade with the Japanese in the late eighteenth and nineteenth centuries, they imported onions – mostly from Bombay. They caught on. In the two years from 1874 onion production in Japan went from 0.06 per cent of total vegetable production to 0.3 per cent.[7] They were easy to grow and suited the climate, and quickly became cheap: by 1906 they could be had for the same price as indigenous taros.[8] The increasing popularity of Westernized dishes also contributed to their rising fortunes in Japan. But they still haven't come close to toppling *negi* as the favourite allium species of the country.

Onions had been introduced to the island of Bermuda in around 1616. Bermuda officially became a British colony in 1707, and the British lost no time in exploiting the potential of their great trade network to make it famous for onions, which quickly became the island's staple crop. They were shipped and sold to Americans on the East Coast, to whom Bermuda was known affectionately as 'Onions' or 'The Onion Patch'. By the end of the nineteenth century, the ss *Trinidad* was carrying more than 30,000 boxes of Bermuda onions to customers in the USA each week, a distance of around 600 miles. Mark Twain, after visiting the island in the late nineteenth century for the magazine *The Atlantic*, wrote in *Some Rambling Notes of an Idle Excursion*:

> The onion is the pride and joy of Bermuda. It is her jewel, her gem of gems. In her conversation, her pulpit, her literature, it is her most frequent and eloquent figure. In Bermuda metaphor it stands for perfection – perfection absolute.
>
> The Bermudian weeping over the departed exhausts praise when he says, 'He was an onion!' The Bermudian extolling the living hero bankrupts applause when he says, 'He is an onion!' The Bermudian setting his son upon the stage of life to dare and do for himself climaxes all counsel, supplication, admonition, comprehends all ambition, when he says, 'Be an onion!'[9]

In 1887 *The Times* of London noted that the onion was the staple crop of Bermuda and informed readers that the Royal Botanic Gardens at Kew were to be informed of any diseases that might be infiltrating the crop;[10] horticulturalists at the Gardens were concerned that any disease could wipe out the economy of the whole island.

Bermuda soon faced competition from American farmers, however; one wily onion grower in Texas developed a variety named 'Bermuda' to compete with the island's produce, reckoning that customers might not read the label too closely before making their purchase. There was even a colony in Texas named Bermuda that capitalized on the popularity

Onions from a 17th-century Japanese herbal, with labels in Old Dutch, Chinese, Japanese and Latin.

The Bermuda onion, from a gardeners' manual of 1894. These onions are little grown commercially these days because of their relatively low yields.

of Bermuda onions in the same way, although it no longer exists. The Bermuda Trade Board tried to stop this tide from turning, sending out postcards to their overseas buyers in the 1930s that read:

> It is the flavour of a genuine 'Bermuda' that is so different. Maybe it is the Sunshine and Sea Breezes down in beautiful Bermuda or some magic in the soil that is responsible, but whatever it is the flavor tells the difference immediately. Be careful then to always look for the crate . . . See that it is marked 'from Bermuda Islands' and you'll know you are getting the real thing.[11]

But their pleas were in vain; in the end, slow shipping by sea became inefficient and made genuine Bermuda onions expensive compared to home-grown produce. Eventually, tourism came to replace onion-growing as the mainstay of the island's economy, although Bermudans still refer to themselves as 'Bermuda onions' to this day.

The British Empire, which covered so much of the globe that it was said that the sun never set on it, also played a part in bringing *A. cepa* varieties around the world. As well as the traditional cuisine they took with them wherever they went, onions featured in a great staple of the British Empire – the bastardized, Anglo-Indian dish known as 'curry' – which eventually found its way to Japan, Southeast Asia, South Africa and the Pacific Islands, furthering the vegetable's spread around the globe.

5
The Modern Allium

Let first the onion flourish there,
Rose among roots, the maiden-fair,
Wine scented and poetic soul,
Of the capacious salad bowl.
Robert Louis Stevenson, 'To a Gardener'

It seems that every country has its own beloved allium dishes and traditions. Britons like them pickled (and you can even buy pickled-onion flavoured crisps), while Koreans favour pickled garlic and New Yorkers love their onion bagels. Chicagoans eat them chopped on hot dogs (but without ketchup), and Mexicans mix sliced spring onions into salads. In Iran, crisp fried onions are a very important part of the cuisine, and home cooks will fry up great quantities in batches, ready for use as garnishes; in Persian cooking, onions are always sliced the same way – into 'new moon' shapes – and when a girl can fry onions perfectly, it is said that she is ready for marriage. But onions haven't always been as appreciated – and celebrated – as they are now. It has taken shortages, global trade, scientific breakthroughs in breeding and the diffusion of different food cultures around the globe for alliums to take their place as one of the most prized vegetable families in the world.

Onions at War

The Times of London reported in the 1920s (with its tongue in its cheek) that the famous activist and vegetarian Mahatma Gandhi and his friends had founded an 'Onion Appreciation Society' in South Africa in the early part of the twentieth century, and a similar one was set up in Kalamazoo, Michigan:

> Why is it, says the society, that smokers have been allowed such latitude with their stale exhalations, which are not regarded as a major or even a minor offence, when the scent of onions is still an affront for which apology is expected? It is, in part, the extraordinary power of the onion to evoke the associations of a whole meal . . . in a dyspeptic and dieting age.
>
> It may not without illegitimate boasting be said that the whole fabric of modern business rests upon onions, for the part they play in providing carbon paper and so enabling business men to recall what they wrote and decided on the previous day . . . the Courts of Law would be lost without it.[1]

They just couldn't understand what the fuss was about – yet. (Incidentally, *The Times* had it wrong on at least one point: onions are not used to make onion-skin paper. The paper is so named for its resemblance to onion skin.) But in Britain onion acreage was declining.

This was despite the fact that people were eating more vegetables as a result of advances in the science of nutrition. The role of vitamins in the diet had been discovered, and for the first time vegetables weren't just considered food for the poor, a substitute or a garnish for meat. However, the advent of the railways meant that farmers could opt to produce cash crops of perishable items such as soft fruit and flowers and send them to markets in London and other big cities, rather than selling cheaper vegetables to locals for a smaller profit. Staple food products were therefore bought in cheaply from abroad instead of being grown at home. *The Times* reported in 1936 that

> Onions obtain no specific [trade] protection in addition to the general [import] duty of 10 per cent, ad valorem, and it is claimed that the severe foreign competition has made it unprofitable to grow a crop which occupies the ground so long and involves such a high expenditure on hand labour.[2]

In 1939, some 98 per cent of the onions sold in Britain had been grown abroad, in places such as France and the Netherlands. Many were sold by travelling 'onion johnnies' from the port of Roscoff in Brittany (where there is still a 'rue des Johnnies'). These bicycling salesmen wore distinctive Breton blue-and-white striped tops and berets and balanced braids of pink onions over their shoulders; they have become a British stereotype of the French that is still seen in cartoons today.

But on the outbreak of the Second World War in 1939, the onion johnnies left the UK's shores, and their onions went with them. *The Times* reported that on 7 September 1939 some 1,600 Frenchmen, recalled to join their regiments, were cheered off from the docks. They included 'onion sellers from Brittany who had been in this country only a few weeks'. All at once the British public realized how often they reached for an onion to bulk up a soup or sweeten a stew. The Ministry of Food advised allotment-holders and amateur gardeners to start growing their own, but it takes some time to grow an onion crop. Such was

Peter Fraser, 'Dig On for Victory' poster, 1942.

Poster by James Montgomery Flagg for the National War Garden Commission, *c.* 1918.

the shortage that the humble vegetable all but disappeared from people's diets, especially in towns. This was partly because a standard price had been set of 4½d. per pound, so there was no advantage to sellers in paying for transportation to different markets if they could sell on their own doorsteps instead.

Angry letters were written to the papers by people who felt bereft. Suddenly, onions were a valuable commodity. In 1940 one specimen, auctioned for charity at a football match, went for £3 1s. 6d., a little under the average weekly wage; today's equivalent might be in the region of £400 ($600). A lady in North Devon offered a field for rent for a year for the price of one onion. One greengrocer, Claude George Crowder, was taken to court and fined £4 plus costs at East Ham for telling a woman that 'she could not have onions without carrots', and charging her 4½d. for one onion and three carrots.[3] There were also stories about people who faced criminal proceedings for having pulled up their seedlings and sold them as spring onions, rather than waiting for the full bulbing onion to crop, a practice that was considered wasteful.

In 1941 the British government bought up a large part of the onion crop of Egypt and announced that much land that had previously been used for farming livestock was to be turned over to the production of vegetables, including 1,500 per cent more onions. Space was reserved especially for the vegetable on the ships that dodged German U-boats to enter British waters with vital supplies. Unfortunately, though, the purchase of the Egyptian crop still allowed only an extra 2 lb of onions for each person in Britain that autumn, a statistic reported indignantly by the press.[4] In that same year a law even came in banning the lifting of onions for spring onions, rather than leaving them in the ground to mature.

The Duke of Norfolk wrote to *The Times* in 1943 suggesting that 'onion clubs' be set up, each of around twenty children who would raise onions on land donated to them. He envisioned that in this way 1,000 clubs could raise 2–3,000 tonnes of onions for the armed forces, whose morale would undoubtedly be improved as a result. 'The onion may not be an essential food like the potato,' he said, 'but it is a most necessary vegetable and is missed more than any other.'[5] Sadly, perhaps because of the unwillingness of farmers to turn over good land rent-free to teams of enthusiastic children, the onion clubs remained only a dream. But onions returned to Britons' diets gradually towards the end of the war as the shortage diminished, and perhaps were more appreciated thereafter than they had been previously.

Poster by Edward Penfield, 1918.

Children's 'victory gardens' in New York, between First Avenue and 35th and 36th streets, 1944.

Onion Hybridization

In the late nineteenth century and early twentieth, new state-funded stations manned by biologists and agricultural scientists were set up by countries around the world. These were aimed at breeding new and improved varieties of grain, fruit and vegetable that could solve the problem of hunger. In this brave new world of agricultural science, food would be more nutritious, easier to grow, more heavily cropping and resistant to disease.

The main scientific development of the twentieth century so far as allium growing is concerned is the ability to produce an F1 hybrid, a way of making sure that one's crop has certain reliable and desirable characteristics such as disease resistance. The process depends on the genetic theory developed by Gregor Mendel in the nineteenth century. Before Mendel, most biologists had held that inherited characteristics were 'blended', meaning that the traits of each parent would be mixed together in their offspring, which would inherit the average of the two. For example, a tall parent and a short parent would produce offspring of medium height. But this theory has some problems, the first being, of course, that this is demonstrably not always the case – sometimes two short parents have tall children. The second problem is that logically, variations would lessen with each generation – if all children were between their two parents in height, within a few generations no one would be particularly tall or short – and that doesn't seem to be the case either. Mendel theorized that some genetic traits were dominant and some recessive, and that offspring received a full set of characteristics (which we now know as alleles) from each parent. The offspring would exhibit the characteristics that were dominant.

Mendel's theories about genetics were not widely adopted until the twentieth century, when they became of great interest to biologists who were developing new plant species. If a species is allowed to breed by itself, many variants will appear, since each plant will have a slightly different mix of genes. But geneticists realized that if they made first-generation crosses of plants, they could very accurately predict the traits they would have, because they would know which mix of dominant and recessive alleles they held. An F1 (or first-generation) hybrid will always run true to type, because each plant's mix of dominant and recessive genes will be the same – and the dominant ones will always win out.

Onions were only the second crop to be developed into F1 hybrids, after corn. Most onion flowers have both male and female parts, and removing the male part to avoid unauthorized fertilization involves carefully cutting out the anthers with tweezers, a time-consuming – and thus expensive – task. But in 1924 Californian scientists found a strain of Italian red onions in their breeding plots at Davis that was female-only and could not self-pollinate, unlike other varieties. This variety – pedigree number 13-53 – was a significant find, as it could be propagated true to type with no danger that it would fertilize itself, throwing up varied offspring. It could be the mother of many varieties of F1 hybrid. Bulbs of it were grown and the best seed-setting plants selected and developed. Eventually, scientists developed a type of male plant that would cross with the females to reproduce the females, which would display none of the characteristics of their male parents; and other types that could be crossed with the females to produce crops that would have the right blend of characteristics to be commercially successful, including resistance to downy mildew, smut, pink root and the dastardly insect thrips. This would lessen the need to use pesticides such as DDT. In 'The Story of Hybrid Onions', a report published by the U.S. Department of Agriculture in 1947, the researchers H. A. Jones and A. E. Clarke enthused:

> Scientists have succeeded in crossing suitable inbred lines of onions and obtained excellent results. One hybrid was more than three times heavier than either parent. Other hybrids were outstanding in shape, size, uniformity, and time of maturity. Even more significant: The results showed great possibilities for using hybrid seed for commercial crop production.

The future of agriculture may have looked bright in the 1950s, when these reliable, disease-resistant, heavy-yielding varieties were first developed, but the worry now among scientists is that the use of F1 hybrids reduces the genetic base of species, leading to a sort of 'genetic erosion'. Fewer and fewer species are now grown commercially. In the USA most of the onions grown today are of three main types: sweet Spanish, which produce large, sweet bulbs; types with white skins that dry well, such as 'White Creole', which are used in dehydrated products; and long-day cultivars that are designed to be kept for a long time.[6] The fear is that as fewer species are grown, one new strain of disease could wipe out a large proportion of the world's onion crop if a commonly grown variety had little resistance to it.[7] Protesters also argue that genetically modified (GM) crops could interbreed with and pollute traditionally reared crops, meaning that old varieties could die out.

Arthur Rothstein, *Grading and Packing Onions in Rice County, Minnesota*, 1939.

Arthur Rothstein, *Onion Field Worker*, Delta Country, Colorado, 1939.

Production Today

Onions are the second most important horticultural crop in the world after tomatoes. Today the country that grows the most dry onions is China, with 22 million tonnes, followed by India, with 15 million, then the USA, Egypt and Iran, according to statistics released by the UN Food and Agriculture Organization. In fact, in 2010 the Indian government banned the export of onions, fearing that high onion prices on the world market would lead to a national shortage – and an electorate discontented with spikes in prices. India is one of the countries of the world in which onions are most popular, although the tables are topped by Libya, where each member of the population ate 33.6 kg (74 lb) of onions on average in 2011. (To compare, the French, whom the British think of as onion lovers, ate just 5.6 kg (12 lb 5 oz) of onions each on average that same year.) The other onion-loving nations of the world are Albania, Tajikistan, Uzbekistan and Algeria.[8]

The green (or spring) onion table, like the garlic table, is still topped by China – with 960,000 tonnes and 18.5 million tonnes respectively – but Japan and South Korea come next, testifying to the popularity of this ingredient in Asian food. Koreans (and Japanese) have a philosophy that a meal should have five colours – green/blue, red, black, yellow and white – and shredded green onions often make up the 'green' part of the meal, as well as flavouring marinades for dishes like *bulgogi* (grilled beef).

Although China grows the most garlic, South Koreans eat more garlic per capita than any other nation in the world: it's estimated at 8 to 10 cloves, or around 55 g (2 oz), per person, per day. The stalks are sometimes eaten as well as the cloves, and garlic is a popular flavour for *cheongju*, a rice wine, as well as foodstuffs. Just to give you an idea of how that quantity compares to other countries, the average American consumption was around 1 kg (2 lb 5 oz) of garlic per person per *year* in 2010, according to the u.s. Department of Agriculture, and around 75 per cent of that was in the form of dehydrated garlic rather than fresh, pungent cloves. Most of the u.s.'s home-grown garlic comes from Gilroy, California, which hosts the annual Gilroy Garlic Festival, but with statistics like this, the town's claim to be the 'garlic capital of the world' may be seen as a little optimistic. However, the relatively low consumption of garlic across the nation has not deterred America from designating 19 April National Garlic Day.

Leeks and other alliaceous vegetables – such as the *negi* so beloved by the Japanese, and the Chinese and Japanese *rakkyo* – are mostly produced by Indonesia, followed by Turkey and France. Japan's favourite alliums, *negi*, themselves come in many different varieties. Some are almost as thick as leeks, while others are thread-thin. The most common variety is perhaps

Mural at Gilroy, California, the self-styled Garlic Capital of the World.

'senju', but there are special local varieties too, such as 'hakata manno', raised on the island of Kyushu. *Negi* are usually served raw on top of soba noodles and accompany *natto* (fermented soy beans) and tofu, and are nearly always found in miso soup, as well as topping noodles or stir-fries with a crisp, green garnish. Strong-smelling foods were traditionally believed to act as a preservative against evil, so *negi* were traditionally given to people who were feeling poorly, or even put in bags around their necks to drive the disease away. Green onions in their many varieties are also used in Korea to flavour kimchi. The USA isn't even among the top twenty leek-producing countries.

Garlic ice cream at the Gilroy Garlic Festival, 2012 – a small cone is enough!

Negi used in *dojo nabe* (loach hotpot), a Japanese fish dish.

Americans do, however, now eat more onions than they ever have before. In 2010 the average American ate 21 lb 6 oz (9.7 kg) of onions each year, up from 19 lb 8 oz (8.8 kg) per person in 1998. This may be because of rising concern with healthy eating and a general trend towards eating more vegetables; a changing demographic in which Latino food cultures, which include lots of onions and garlic, are becoming more significant; or, conversely, for the more pessimistic, because of the ever-increasing popularity of hamburgers, which generally come with an onion garnish!

Modern Industrial Processes

Nowadays the onion added to your package of hamburgers or the garlic in your carton of soup from the chiller cabinet may not be as nature intended. Modern industrial processes have been developed to improve ingredients' shelf life and make

Onion rings, battered and deep-fried.

them easier to transport, as well as to concentrate flavour. Onions and garlic can be steam-distilled to create highly flavoured oils which can be added to soups and other prepared dishes, which means that the flavour is retained, but the fibre – and many of the nutrients – is lost. Alternatively, they may undergo the process of dehydration.

Drying is a very old method of preservation – in 1700 BCE the Assyrian Gimil-Marduk wrote to his superior asking for a basket of garlic that had been dried outside in the sun[9] – but modern industrial dehydration starts with the onions being skinned and then topped and tailed, sterilized, washed and chopped or sliced. The prepared onions are then dried in hot air, starting at 75°C (165°F) and decreasing to 60°C (140°F) as the moisture content declines. If this is done too quickly, they may caramelize and darken. After being dried out with a final blast of hot air, they're ready when the moisture content reaches just 4 per cent. A similar process can be undergone by garlic. Sometimes the dried-out cloves are left as flakes; otherwise they can be ground to a powder and used in ketchup, mayonnaise, stocks, soups and snacks, or added to salt to flavour it. A paste made from the dried onion powder plus starch and salt might be extruded into 'onion rings', those crispy little rings you can buy in shakers to sprinkle on top of your salads and burgers.[10] The usa is one of the world's largest markets for these concentrated onion and garlic products.

Tears

As any cook knows, the onion has its own defence mechanism: making you cry. The ability of the onion to stimulate tears means that in Yiddish the 'crocodile tears' cried by an insincere person are known as 'onion tears' instead. 'I, an ass, am onion-eyed', says Mark Antony's close friend Enobarbus in Shakespeare's *Antony and Cleopatra* (iv.v), meaning that he has been moved to tears. How exactly the onion does this is still the subject of scientific research, and in 2013 the Ig Nobel Prize for Chemistry was handed to a team of Japanese researchers who had worked out how onions make you cry. Their paper, published in *Nature*, reports:

> The irritating lachrymatory factor that is released by onions when they are chopped up has been presumed to be produced spontaneously following the action of the enzyme alliinase, which operates in the biochemical pathway that produces the compounds responsible for

the onion's characteristic flavour. Here we show that this factor is not formed as a by-product of this reaction, but that it is specifically synthesized by a previously undiscovered enzyme, lachrymatory-factor synthase. It may be possible to develop a non-lachrymatory onion that still retains its characteristic flavour and high nutritional value by downregulating the activity of this synthase enzyme.[11]

In layman's terms, when you cut into an onion, you break some of its cells, which release substances that form a volatile gas that permeates the air, combining with the moisture in your eyes to form sulphuric acid. The sulphuric acid leads to a burning sensation, and tears are produced in the tear glands in order to wash the irritant away.

One powerful image of onion tears comes in Günter Grass's novel *The Tin Drum* (1959), whose anti-hero and unreliable narrator Oskar Matzerath, a young man from Danzig (now Gdansk, Poland), lives through the Second World War and the postwar reconstruction of Europe. He tells of the nightclub The Onion Cellar, an expensive and high-class establishment frequented by well-off types who sit uncomfortably on onion sacks, waiting for the main event of the evening to get under way. It is just after the war, and the people of Germany are suffering a crisis: 'These people wanted to talk, to unburden themselves, but they couldn't seem to get started; despite all their efforts, they left the essential unsaid, talked around it.' Unable to face the horrors they have seen, they cannot talk, or cry. The club's proprietor dons a shawl decorated with onions and, with great showmanship, brings out chopping boards and paring knives and presents them to the clientele. 'Ladies and gentlemen, help yourselves!', he calls. And they do.

Anti-onion gas mask at Camp Kearny, California, *c.* 1942.

> What did the onion juice do? It did what the world and the sorrows of the world could not do: it brought forth a round, human tear. It made them cry. At last they were able to cry again. To cry properly, without restraint, to cry like mad. The tears flowed and washed everything away.

These lucky survivors feel they must pay for the privilege of having emotion teased out of them in a safe setting, so damaged are they by their experiences.

In purely physical terms, some people are more sensitive than others to the onion's secret weapon, but if you are one of these unfortunates, there are a few tried-and-tested methods for avoiding the pain. One is to keep your onions in the refrigerator, since if they are cold, their chemistry changes and the release of the compound will be slowed. Cutting the onions under water will also help, as will wearing contact lenses, glasses or even special onion goggles, designed to help those most sensitive (and stylish?) of choppers. It's also reported that using a really sharp, thin knife will reduce tears, since a very precise cut will break fewer of the cell walls, thus releasing less of the irritant. But if you're really desperate, there is hope: a new genetically modified 'tearless onion' has been developed by scientists in New Zealand. Perhaps some time in the twenty-first century, onion tears will become a distant memory.

Onion Breath

In Shakespeare's *A Midsummer Night's Dream*, Bottom pleads with his fellow actors: 'most dear actors, eat no onions nor garlic, for we are to utter sweet breath; and I do not doubt but to hear them say, it is a sweet comedy.' (Even now it is a well-known practical joke among actors to eat onions before

Gerrit Dou, *Girl Chopping Onions*, 1646.

kissing scenes in order to put off their co-stars.) Onions and garlic are notorious for making the breath of people who eat them smell. The problem is allicin, which is broken down into various sulphur-containing compounds as the garlic or onion goes through the digestive process. One of these compounds, allyl methyl sulphide, takes a long time to break down, which means that the odour of garlic will stick around for some time after you have eaten it. It travels to the lungs, kidneys and skin to be excreted. That's why breath mints and mouthwash aren't terribly effective against the smell, which can suffuse your whole body. The traditional remedy is to eat parsley or mint, but no scientific study has ever proved the effectiveness of either. However, help may be at hand: in 2010 Sheryl Barringer and Areerat Hansanugrum of Ohio State University published a study that demonstrated that drinking a glass of milk helps to dissipate the aroma. Apparently the mixture of fat and water helps to alleviate the smell. Those who wish to test this theory should note that drinking milk at the same time as eating the garlic worked better than drinking a glass of milk after the meal.[12]

Nutrition

Garlic and onions are still sold as a panacea by makers of health supplements. Garlic pills are one of the most popular supplements, supposed to do everything from reducing cholesterol and helping the subject avoid heart disease, to curing colds – and all without giving you smelly breath. The jury is still out on their effectiveness, however. A study of 2007 published in the *Archives of Internal Medicine* found that garlic did not reduce blood cholesterol levels in patients with moderately high baseline levels, and Heart.org concluded:

> despite decades of research suggesting that garlic can improve cholesterol profiles, a new NIH [National Institutes of Health]-funded trial found absolutely no effects of raw garlic or garlic supplements on LDL, HDL, or triglycerides. The findings underscore the hazards of meta-analyses made up of small, flawed studies and the value of rigorously studying popular herbal remedies.

It's also worth noting that although there is some evidence that onion juice can help to heal cuts and fight infection, and that it can kill cancerous cells, this has been observed only in certain laboratory tests; the results cannot necessarily be applied to what happens within the human digestive system. In addition, the *New York Times* reported in 2002 that a study had shown that of the fourteen garlic supplements then on the market, seven contained less of the active ingredient than researchers consider necessary for the supplement to have the advertised effect on the human body.[13] Buyer beware!

That being said, eating onions and garlic themselves, rather than supplements, is very obviously good for you. They are high in vitamin C, vitamin B6 and folic acid, and are a good source of fibre. The World Health Organization recommends onions for coughs, colds, asthma and bronchitis, just as Traditional Chinese Medicine does. Studies have shown that people who eat a lot of garlic and other alliums are less likely to suffer from stomach, breast, oesophageal, colorectal, prostate or intestinal cancer. Alliums contain natural antioxidants, prebiotics (which help with digestion) and the compounds quercetin and chromium, which are supposed to be anti-inflammatory (and possibly helpful for hay fever sufferers) and good for hormone balance respectively.

The amount of methane gas emitted by cows is also reduced if they are fed onions and garlic, although unfortunately they also taint the taste of the milk when fed to cows in their raw form; research is therefore being carried out into supplementing the feed of cows with some allium derivative. Perhaps in this way, the allium family might help to slow the process of climate change – although reducing our consumption of meat and dairy products would be a more efficient way to do it.

Smuggling and Other Crimes

The past few years have seen an increase in a new and unexpected kind of crime: garlic smuggling. In the EU a 9.6 per cent customs duty is levied on imports of foreign garlic, which is intended to protect European garlic growers from being undercut by Chinese farmers. There is also an additional charge of €1,200 per tonne. This has led to a huge rise in underhand practices in the garlic industry, and in 2013 Sweden issued an international arrest warrant for two Britons believed to be masterminding a €10 million smuggling ring in which garlic went via Norway, which as a non-EU state has no garlic tariff, into Sweden and the EU without being declared. Other crimes include labelling garlic as other produce in order to avoid the bill. In December 2012 a man from west London was convicted of smuggling garlic into the country disguised as ginger, which is not subject to the levy, and thus avoiding a £2.5 million ($4 million) tax bill. One wonders whether the smell was what tipped off Customs.[14]

Fairs and Festivals

Though the onion fairs once seen throughout Britain have diminished, there are still plenty of celebrations of the onion worldwide. Onion fairs are held as far apart as Maui and Mumbai. The Onion Fayre held in the Forest of Dean in Gloucestershire, England, dates back to the thirteenth century: prizes are given for onion growing, and an onion-eating competition is held in which ladies must eat a 5-oz (140-g) peeled onion and men a 7-oz (200-g) specimen. The winning times in 2012 were 1 minute 24 seconds and 1 minute

6 seconds, respectively. All entrants are welcome, and are advised to bring their own mouthwash.

The Zwiebelfest (onion festival) of Esslingen am Neckar, Germany, is held every August, but the most famous onion fair in Germany may be the Zwiebelmarkt in Weimar, a three-day event during which residents decorate their houses with onion garlands. The first recorded mention of it dates from 1653, when it was described as 'a market for beasts and onions'. Its most famous attendant was the poet Goethe (1749–1832), who is said to have decorated his desk – and his house – with plaited onion hearts in honour of the festival. Every October it welcomes over 350,000 onion lovers. Girls and young women who live in Weimar or the surrounding area can apply for the position of 'onion queen', the face of the festival, which is awarded to a new candidate every year.

Calçots cooking over a charcoal fire, Catalonia, Spain. The correct way to eat a calçot is to hold it by the green end and lower it into the mouth.

This erotic postcard from Berlin of around 1901 shows a nude girl rising from an onion bulb. *Rüdige Bolle* roughly means 'naughty bulb' and was a slang term for a cheeky or fast person.

Allium ursinum, also known as wild garlic and ramsons. The name means 'bear's garlic', since brown bears are believed to dig up the bulbs and eat them.

Catalonia is Spain is the home of the calçot, a mild, less bulbous form of resprouted onion that looks rather like a giant spring onion. In *calçotada* festivals, held between December and March, calçots are charred over hot fires and served with a special sauce made by pounding together hazelnuts, garlic, vinegar, breadcrumbs, tomatoes and chilli. After the locals have gorged on calçots, local sausages are cooked on the fires, and the traditional end to the feast is a dessert of oranges.[15]

But *Allium cepa* isn't the only kind of allium to get its own festival: the Isle of Wight holds a yearly Garlic Festival; Calhoun, West Virginia, holds a Ramps Festival every year; the chef Michael Städtlander holds a Wild Leek and Maple Syrup Festival at his farm in Ontario; and in Vlaardingen in the Netherlands, there's a Rock 'n' Ramps Festival where one can eat ramps-flavoured dishes and listen to rock bands.

Recipes

Historical Recipes

Vegetable Dinner, Easily Digested
From *Apicius*, or *De re coquinaria*

All green vegetables are suited for this purpose. Very young beet-root and well-matured leeks are parboiled; arrange them in a baking dish, grind pepper and cumin, add broth and condensed must, or anything else to sweeten them a little, heat and finish them on a slow fire, and serve.

Pea and Onion Soup for Fish Days
From *Le Ménagier de Paris*, trans. Janet Hinson

On a fish day, when the peas are cooked, you should have onions which have been cooked as long as the peas in a pot and like the bacon cooked separately in another pot, and as with the bacon water you may nourish and serve the peas, in the same way; on fish days, when you have put your peas on the fire in a pot, you must put aside your minced onions in another pot, and with onion water serve and nourish the peas; and when all is cooked fry the onions and put half of them in the peas, and the other half in the liquid from the peas of which I spoke above, and then add salt. And if on this fish day or in Lent there is salted whale-meat, you must do with the whale-meat as with the bacon on a meat day.

Potage Maigre

From John Evelyn, *Acetaria: A Discourse of Sallets* (1699)

Take four Quarts of Spring-Water, two or three Onions stuck with some Cloves, two or three Slices of Limon Peel, Salt, whole white Pepper, Mace, a Raze or two of Ginger, tied up in a fine Cloth (Lawn or Tiffany) and make all boil for half an Hour; Then having Spinage, Sorrel, white Beet-Chard, a little Cabbage, a few small Tops of Cives, wash'd and pick'd clean, shred them well, and cast them into the Liquor, with a Pint of blue Pease boil'd soft and strain'd, with a Bunch of sweet Herbs, the Top and Bottom of a French Roll; and so suffer it to boil during three Hours; and then dish it with another small French Roll, and Slices about the Dish: Some cut Bread in slices, and frying them brown (being dried) put them into the Pottage just as it is going to be eaten.

The same Herbs, clean wash'd, broken and pulled asunder only, being put in a close cover'd Pipkin, without any other Water or Liquor, will stew in their own Juice and Moisture. Some add an whole Onion, which after a while should be taken out, remembering to season it with Salt and Spice, and serve it up with Bread and a Piece of fresh Butter.

Sausages after the German Way

From Hannah Glasse, *The Art of Cookery Made Plain and Easy* (1747)

These economical sausages made mostly from bread and offal ('lights' are lungs) demonstrate the traditional matching of cheap meat, or stuffing, with onion.

Take the crumb of a two-penny loaf, one pound of suet, half a lamb's lights, a handful of parsley, some thyme, marjory, and onion; mince all very small; then season with salt and pepper. These must be stuffed in a sheep's gut; they are fried in oil or melted suet, and are only fit for immediate use.

To Make an Onion Pye
From Hannah Glasse, *The Art of Cookery Made Plain and Easy* (1747)

This pie is notable for its huge quantity of nutmeg, as well as the blend of sweet apples and savoury vegetables.

Wash and pare some potatoes, and cut them in slices, peel some onions, cut them in slices, pare some apples and slice them, make a good crust, cover your dish, lay a quarter of a pound of butter all over, take a quarter of an ounce of mace beat fine, a nutmeg grated, a tea-spoonful of beaten pepper, three tea-spoonfuls of salt, mix all together, strew some over the butter, lay a layer of potatoes, a layer of onions, a layer of apples and a layer of eggs, and so on till you have filled your pie, strewing a little of the seasoning between each layer, and a quarter of a pound of butter in bits, and six spoonfuls of water. Close your pie, and bake it an hour and a half. A pound of potatoes, a pound of onions, a pound of apples, and twelve eggs will do.

Pickled Onions
From *Mrs Beeton's Book of Household Management* (1861)

1 gallon of pickling onions, salt and water, milk; to each ½ gallon of vinegar, 1 oz of bruised ginger, ¼ teaspoonful of cayenne, 1 oz of allspice, 1 oz of whole black pepper, ¼ oz of whole nutmeg bruised, 8 cloves, ¼ oz of mace.

Gather the onions, which should not be too small, when they are quite dry and ripe; wipe off the dirt, but do not pare them; make a strong solution of salt and water, into which put the onions, and change this, morning and night, for 3 days, and save the last brine they were put in. Then take the outside skin off, and put them into a tin saucepan capable of holding them all, as they are always better done together. Now take equal quantities of milk and the last salt and water the onions were in, and pour this to them; to this add 2 large spoonfuls of salt, put them over the fire, and watch them very attentively. Keep constantly turning the onions about with a wooden skimmer, those at the bottom to the top, and vice versâ; and let the milk and water run through the holes of the skimmer. Remember, the onions must never boil, or, if they do, they will be good for nothing; and they should be quite transparent. Keep the onions stirred for a few minutes, and, in stirring them, be particular not to break them. Then have ready a pan with a colander, into which turn the onions to drain, covering them with a cloth to keep in the steam. Place on a table an old cloth, 2 or 3 times double; put the onions on it when quite hot, and over them an old piece of blanket; cover this closely over them, to keep in the steam. Let them remain till the next day, when they will be quite cold, and look yellow and shrivelled; take off the shrivelled skins, when they should be as white as snow. Put them in a pan, make a pickle of vinegar and the remaining ingredients, boil all these up, and pour hot over the onions in the pan. Cover very closely to keep in all the steam, and let them stand till the following day, when they will be quite cold. Put them into jars or bottles well bunged, and a tablespoonful of the best olive-oil on the top of each jar or bottle. Tie them down with bladder, and let them stand in a cool place for a month or six weeks, when they will be fit for use. They should be beautifully white, and eat crisp, without the least softness, and will keep good many months. Seasonable from the middle of July to the end of August.

Modern Recipes

French Onion Soup

75 g butter
4 onions, sliced thinly
1 tbsp plain (all-purpose) flour
2 sprigs thyme
750 ml beef stock
250 ml light French (hard) cider
1 tbsp balsamic vinegar
8 slices baguette, around 1.5 cm thick
100 g grated Gruyère

Melt the butter in a large pan. Add the onions and cook over a low heat until caramelized – around an hour and a half. If you want to speed up the process, add a pinch of brown sugar, but don't oversweeten.

When the onions are dark brown all through and soft, stir in the flour and thyme. When it's combined so there are no lumps, add the liquid. Keep stirring while you bring it to the boil, then take it down to a simmer and cook for an hour.

Season. Toast the bread slices until golden on each side. Ladle the soup into four ovenproof bowls and top each with two slices of toasted baguette and a quarter of the grated cheese. Put the bowls under the grill until the cheese is melted and bubbling.

Serves 4

Gao Choi Gau (Prawn and Chive Dumplings)

These classic dim sum are quite easy to make. Use Chinese garlic chives if you can get them.

For the gao choi gau
200 g raw prawns (shrimp), minced
200 g chives or garlic chives, finely chopped
1 egg white
1 clove garlic, minced
1 tsp cornflour
2 tsp shaoxing wine
1 tsp sesame oil
1 tsp caster (superfine) sugar
½ tsp salt
24 dumpling skins

For the dipping sauce
3 tbsp soy sauce
3 tbsp rice vinegar
½ tsp sesame oil
1 pinch dried red chilli flakes

Mix together the ingredients for the filling and put a teaspoon of it in the centre of each skin. Fold the skins in half with the seam at the top, so they look a bit like Cornish pasties. Steam in a bamboo steamer for 6–7 minutes, combine the ingredients for the dipping sauce and serve.

Beef Negimaki

This Japanese dish from the Kantō region is great served with a honey-ginger sauce.

4 *negi* (or bunching onions, if you can't find *negi*), cut into
4-cm pieces

350 g rump or sirloin steak, cut into strips 5 cm by 3.5 cm
and around 1 cm thick
60 ml soy sauce
2 tsp peanut (groundnut) oil
2 tbsp honey
1 clove garlic, minced
1 inch ginger, minced

Wrap the strips of steak around the *negi*. Thread them on to bamboo skewers so they stay wrapped up. Grill for 5 minutes on each side, turning halfway through. Mix the rest of the ingredients together to make a dipping sauce and serve.

Korean Pickled Garlic

Adapted from Hyosun Ro, www.koreanbapsang.com

The garlic becomes sweeter and less overpowering during the two-step pickling process.

900 g garlic (about 16 heads)
550 ml rice vinegar
1 tbsp sea salt
1.2 l water
300 ml soy sauce
70 g caster (superfine) sugar

Pull the garlic cloves from the heads and soak them in hot water so the skins come off easily. Remove the skins and cut off the woody part at the bottom. Put the drained cloves in sterilized jars.

Make the first pickling liquid by mixing together 300 ml of the rice vinegar, the salt and 600 ml of the water. Pour it over the garlic, covering all the cloves, put the lids on and leave to rest at room temperature for five days.

Empty out the garlic into a bowl, draining off the liquid. Wash and re-sterilize the jars. Bring the rest of the water and rice vinegar, together with the soy sauce and sugar, to the boil and cook for 3–4 minutes. Allow to cool slightly while you put the garlic cloves back into the jars. Pour the soy sauce mixture over the top, submerging the garlic, put the lids on and leave for at least two weeks before you start to eat it.

Jewish Onion Rolls

These are popular in Jewish bakeries in New York. Some recipes use dehydrated onions for the topping, which are left to soak in the warm water that is then used for the dough. The resulting topping isn't as gutsy as in the recipe below, but the aroma of onion permeates the whole roll.

500 g strong white bread flour
2 tsp sugar
1½ tsp salt
1 packet yeast
240 ml warm water
3 tbsp vegetable oil
1 large, sweet onion, chopped finely
1 tbsp poppy seeds
1 egg, beaten

Mix together the flour, sugar, half a teaspoon of salt and the yeast. Pour the water and 2 tbsp of the oil into a well in the centre and gradually combine it into a dough. Knead for 8–10 minutes until the dough is silky. Form into a ball and leave, in a clean bowl covered with a clean, damp cloth, in a warm place for an hour, or until it has doubled in size.

Divide the dough into eight pieces and form into rolls. Leave to rise on a floured, greased baking sheet. It should take around half an hour. While the rolls are rising, fry the onion in the remaining oil with the last teaspoon of salt. Add the poppy seeds.

When the rolls are risen, egg-wash them and sprinkle the onion mixture on top. Bake for around 15–20 minutes or until they sound hollow when tapped on the bottom.

Lamb Dopiaza

1 kg lamb shoulder, cut into chunks
3 tbsp vegetable oil
3 large onions, chopped
3 tsp coriander seeds
3 tsp cumin seeds
2 tsp garam masala
1 tsp turmeric
5-cm piece fresh ginger made into a paste with 3 cloves garlic
3 chopped tomatoes (or half a tin)
350 ml water
salt and pepper

First brown the lamb in the oil, then remove it from the pan. Fry two-thirds of the onions in the same pan until soft. Add the spices and fry for a couple of minutes until they release their aromas. Put the lamb back in, together with the ginger and garlic paste and tomatoes, and cook for a couple of minutes before adding the last third of the onions. Sauté for 3 or 4 minutes before adding the water and leaving to cook for 40 minutes or until the meat is tender. Season to taste.

Serves 6

Toad in the Hole with Onion Gravy

You can either make servings of this classic British dish individually in Yorkshire pudding tins, or bake the whole thing in one big tin. It's a perfect dish for Bonfire Night or Halloween.

For the toad in the hole:
2 tsp vegetable oil
75 g plain (all-purpose) flour
1 egg
130 ml semi-skimmed (half-fat) milk
6 good-quality sausages (these are the 'toads')

For the onion gravy:
2 medium-sized onions, sliced very thinly
2 tsp vegetable oil
1 tsp caster (superfine) sugar
1 tsp mustard powder
around 2 tsp plain (all-purpose) flour
1 tsp balsamic vinegar
300 ml beef stock

Turn the oven on to 220°C (425°F) to heat. Add the oil to your metal tin (or tins) and put in the oven, then start to get the batter ready. Sift the flour into a bowl and break the egg into a hollow in the centre. Start to whisk the two together. When they are blended, add the milk and blend further until smooth. Leave to stand.

Now the oven is heated, add your sausages to the tin. They should sizzle in the oil. Stir them around a bit so they sear briefly. Put them back in the oven for ten minutes to give them a chance to get going.

Check that the bottom of the tin is coated with oil from the sausages. If they were quite lean, you might need to add another small splash of vegetable oil over low heat to coat the tin so that the batter doesn't stick. Make sure the sausages are evenly spaced and pour the batter around them, watching it sizzle. Put back in the oven for half an hour.

While it's cooking, make the onion gravy. Cook the onions very slowly in the oil over low heat with the sugar, stirring constantly, until they are brown and caramelized. Add the mustard powder and flour and stir until blended, then the balsamic vinegar. When that's all blended smoothly, add the stock. Blend and keep simmering until it thickens and goes silky.

The 'hole' will puff up in the oven and the 'toads' will stick out invitingly. Somehow the slightly burned tips of sausages just work in this dish. Serve with mashed potatoes, peas and mustard or ketchup.

Serves 2 greedy people

Red Eggs

These eggs are traditionally made for Easter in Greece. The red colour of the eggs symbolizes the blood of Christ. It may seem odd that eggs can be dyed using yellow onion skins, but it works!

skins of 8 Spanish onions
1 tbsp white wine vinegar
500 ml water
6 eggs

Boil up the onion skins in the vinegar and water and simmer for 30 minutes. Strain into a bowl and let cool. Don't use a porous bowl that might get stained – Pyrex would be good.

Put the eggs in the bottom of a pan and pour the dye over the top. Bring to the boil, then simmer for 15 minutes. Strain.

You can polish up these eggs with a little olive oil to make them shine.

Cebollitas

These Mexican grilled spring onions, cooked on a barbecue so they blacken slightly, are closely related to the calçots of Spain.

1 bunch fat spring onions (scallions)
2 tbsp olive oil
juice of 2 limes
coriander (cilantro)

Clean the spring onions and toss them in the oil and lime juice to cover them lightly. Remove from the dressing, season with salt and grill on a barbecue for 1 to 2 minutes on each side, until they're softened. Pour any remaining dressing over the top and garnish with the coriander.

Spaghetti Aglio e Olio

This classic Italian recipe is super-simple and delicious. It's a perfect snack at the end of an evening out and can be prepared very quickly. The most important thing to remember is not to burn the garlic!

500 g spaghetti
6 cloves garlic, very thinly sliced
120 ml extra-virgin olive oil
½ tsp dried chilli flakes
30 g chopped flat-leaf parsley
90 g grated Parmesan

Bring a large pot of salted water to the boil and throw in the pasta. Warm the olive oil in a large frying pan and add the garlic and chilli flakes. Don't let the oil get too hot or the garlic will burn. It should only be golden, not brown. Once it's golden, add three tablespoonfuls of the pasta water to the oil so the garlic stops browning.

When the spaghetti is cooked, drain it and add it to the garlicky oil. Add the parsley and Parmesan and toss. Serve straight away.
Serves 4

References

Introduction

1 Mario Ledwith, 'Now That's Eye-watering! Gardener Produces Onion Weighing 18 lb and Smashes World Record', *Mail Online*, 14 September 2012, www.dailymail.co.uk.
2 J. L. Brewster, *Onions and Other Vegetable Alliums* (Wallingford, 2008), p. 17.
3 Ibid., p. 20.
4 Ibid., p. 14.
5 Alan Davidson, 'Welsh Onion', *The Oxford Companion to Food* (London, 2010).

1 The Ancient Allium

1 Jean Bottéro, *The Oldest Cuisine in the World*, trans. Teresa Lavender Fagan (Chicago, IL, 2004), p. 69.
2 Ibid., p. 26.
3 Joan P. Alcock, *Food in the Ancient World* (Westport, CT, 2006), p. 53.
4 Ibid.
5 Ibid.
6 Andrew Dalby, *Food in the Ancient World from A to Z* (London and New York, 2003), p. 193.

7 Ibid.
8 Ibid., p. 155.

2 The Medieval Onion

1 C. Anne Wilson, *Food and Drink in Britain from the Stone Age to Recent Times* (London, 1973), p. 197.
2 Ibid., p. 203.
3 Ibid., p. 85.
4 Ibid., p. 197.
5 D. C. Watts, 'Leek', *Dictionary of Plant Lore* (Burlington, San Diego and London, 2007).
6 Hannele Klemettilä, *The Medieval Kitchen: A Social History with Recipes* (London, 2012), p. 39.

3 Travel, Trade and Folklore

1 Marian Coonse, *Onions, Leeks and Garlic: A Handbook for Gardeners* (College Station, TX, 1995), p. 6.
2 Eric Block, *Garlic and Other Alliums: The Myth and the Science* (Cambridge, 2010), p. 231.
3 Raphael [pseud.], *The Book of Dreams: Being a Concise Interpretation of Dreams* (Foulsham, n.d. [18??]), cited in D. C. Watts, 'Onion', *Dictionary of Plant Lore* (Burlington, San Diego and London, 2007).
4 Watts, 'Onion'.
5 '"Put Garlic in your Windows and Crosses in your Homes": Serbian Council Warns Residents Vampire is on the Loose after his House Collapses', *Daily Mail*, 27 November 2012.

4 The Onion Improves

1 Marian Coonse, *Onions, Leeks and Garlic:
   A Handbook for Gardeners* (College Station, TX, 1995),
   pp. 6–7.
2 'Royal Horticultural Society', *The Times*, 26 October 1887.
3 'Birmingham Onion Fair', *Illustrated London News*,
   5 October 1872.
4 James Greenwood, *In Strange Company: Being the
   Experiences of a Roving Correspondent* (London, 1874),
   at www.victorianlondon.org.
5 'Birmingham Onion Fair'.
6 'The French Peasant-farmers' Seed Fund', *The Times*,
   24 May 1871.
7 Katarzyna J. Cwiertka, *Modern Japanese Cuisine: Food, Power
   and National Identity* (London, 2006), pp. 102–8.
8 Ibid.
9 'Rise and Fall of the Bermuda Onion', www.bernews.com,
   25 January 2012.
10 'Royal Horticultural Society'.
11 'Rise and Fall of the Bermuda Onion'.

5 The Modern Allium

1 'The Onion Anti-defamation Society', *The Times*,
   7 December 1936.
2 'Vegetable Growing', *The Times*, 13 January 1936.
3 'News in Brief', *The Times*, 17 January 1941.
4 '2 lb of Onions a Head', *The Times*, 20 August 1941.
5 Letter to the Editor [from the Duke of Norfolk], *The Times*,
   27 January 1943.
6 J. L. Brewster, *Onions and Other Vegetable Alliums*
   (Wallingford, 2008), p. 13.
7 Ibid.
8 Food and Agriculture Organization of the United Nations,
   www.faostat.com, accessed 28 January 2015.

9 Jean Bottéro, *The Oldest Cuisine in the World*, trans. Teresa Lavender Fagan (Chicago, IL, 2004), p. 57.

10 Brewster, *Onions and Other Vegetable Alliums*.

11 S. Imai et al., 'Plant Biochemistry: An Onion Enzyme that Makes the Eyes Water', *Nature*, CLXIX/685 (17 October 2002), at www.nature.com.

12 'Drinking a Glass of Milk Can Stop Garlic Breath', www.bbc.co.uk/news, 31 August 2010.

13 John O'Neil, 'Vital Signs: Testing; Something Amiss in the Garlic', *New York Times*, 29 October 2002.

14 'Who, What, Why: Why Do Criminals Smuggle Garlic?', www.bbc.co.uk/news, 12 January 2013.

15 Xanthe Clay, 'The Allure of the Allium', *Daily Telegraph*, 12 February 2012.

Bibliography

Alcock, Joan P., *Food in the Ancient World* (Westport, CT, 2006)

Apicius, *De re coquinaria*, trans. Walter M. Hill,
www.penelope.uchicago.edu

Block, Eric, *Garlic and Other Alliums: The Myth and the Science*
(Cambridge, 2010)

Bottéro, Jean, *The Oldest Cuisine in the World*, trans. Teresa
Lavender Fagan (Chicago, IL, 2004)

Brewster, J. L., *Onions and Other Vegetable Alliums*
(Wallingford, 2008)

Coonse, Marian, *Onions, Leeks and Garlic: A Handbook for
Gardeners* (College Station, TX, 1995)

Cwiertka, Katarzyna J., *Modern Japanese Cuisine: Food, Power
and National Identity* (London, 2006)

Dalby, Andrew, *Food in the Ancient World from A to Z*
(London and New York, 2003)

Davidson, Alan, *The Oxford Companion to Food* (London, 2010)

Evelyn, John, *Acetaria: A Discourse of Sallets* (1699),
at www.gutenberg.org

Homer, *The Iliad*, trans. Samuel Butler, www.perseus.tufts.edu

Jay, Martha, 'Onions at War', *The Foodie Bugle*, 28 August 2012,
www.thefoodiebugle.com

Klemettilä, Hannele, *The Medieval Kitchen: A Social History with
Recipes* (London, 2012)

Laurioux, Bruno, *Manger au Moyen Âge: pratiques et discours
alimentaires en Europe au XIVe et XVe siècles* (Paris, 2002)

Li Ji, trans. James Legge, www.ctext.org

Mayhew, Henry, *London Labour and the London Poor*
    (London, 1851)

Pettid, Michael J., *Korean Cuisine: An Illustrated History* (London,
    2008)

Pliny the Elder, *The Natural History*, trans. John C. Bostock,
    www.perseus.tufts.edu

Shaida, Margaret, *The Legendary Cuisine of Persia* (London, 2004)

Watts, D. C., *Dictionary of Plant Lore* (Burlington, San Diego
    and London, 2007)

Wilson, C. Anne, *Food and Drink in Britain from the Stone Age to
    Recent Times* (London, 1973)

Wujastyk, Dominik, *The Roots of Ayurveda*
    (Harmondsworth, 2003)

Websites and Associations

Black Garlic
www.blackgarlic.com

British Leeks
www.britishleeks.co.uk

British Onions
www.britishonions.co.uk

The Garlic Farm
www.thegarlicfarm.co.uk

Gilroy Garlic Festival
www.gilroygarlic.com

Grow Your Own Garlic and Grow Your Own Onions
www.rhs.org.uk

La Maison des Johnnies et de l'Oignon de Roscoff
The museum of the Onion Johnnies in Roscoff, Brittany
www.roscoff-tourisme.com

The National Onion Association (USA)
www.onions-usa.com

Onions Australia
www.onionsaustralia.org.au

Weimar Onion Fair
www.germany.travel

Photo Acknowledgements

The author and publishers wish to express their thanks to the below sources of illustrative material and/or permission to reproduce it.

The British Museum, London, photos © Trustees of the British Museum: pp. 18, 19, 22, 23, 39, 46, 53; iStock.com/AWEvans: p. 6; The J. Paul Getty Museum, Villa Collection, Malibu, California: p. 27; Library of Congress, Prints and Photographs Division, Washington, DC: pp. 8, 25, 54, 56, 88, 90, 91, 94, 95, 103; The Victoria & Albert Museum, London: pp. 58, 61, 110; The Walters Art Museum, Baltimore: pp. 49, 52, 74; Wellcome Library, London: pp. 13, 37, 41, 50, 81; Yale Center for British Art: p. 40.

AnnaKika, the copyright holder of the image on p. 111, Ayleen Gaspar, the copyright holder of the image on p. 97, M a n u e l, the copyright holder of the image on p. 12, Mpellegr, the copyright holder of the image on p. 109, Anita Ritenour, the copyright holder of the image on p. 98, Umberto Salvagnin, the copyright holder of the image on p. 11, and Kate Ter Haar, the copyright holder of the image on p. 100, have published them online under conditions imposed by a Creative Commons Attribution 2.0 Generic license; Peter Bond, the copyright holder of the image on p. 55, Ivva, the copyright holder of the image on p. 99, and Matt Lavin, the copyright holder of the image on p. 47, have published them online under conditions imposed by a Creative Commons Attribution-Share Alike 2.0 Generic license.

Readers are free:

- to share – to copy, distribute and transmit these images alone
- to remix – to adapt these images alone

Under the following conditions:

- attribution – readers must attribute the images in the manner specified by their authors or licensors (but not in any way that suggests that these parties endorse them or their use of the work).

Index

italic numbers refer to illustrations; **bold** to recipes